The Best Kept Secrets of Parma,

"The Garden City"

A Study of Parma's Streets and the Ridgewood Community

By

Robert Horley

Published with the support of
City of Parma, Ohio
Parma Area Historical Society
Parma Area Chamber of Commerce

A Tribute to

H. A. Stahl

And a Brief Study of His Work

Publisher: Robert Horley
Manuscript Editors: Richard Charnigo, Richard Charnigo, Jr.
                         and Rosemary G. Lenc
Computer Advisor: Rev. Ray J. Horley
Printer: Cowgill Printing Company

Cover Photo: Aerial view of Ridgewood Country Club, Parma, Ohio,
                         summer of 1992. (Used with the permission of Ridgewood
                         Country Club.)

The author wishes to acknowledge the support of the City of Parma, Ohio; the
Parma Area Historical Society; and the Parma Area Chamber of Commerce.

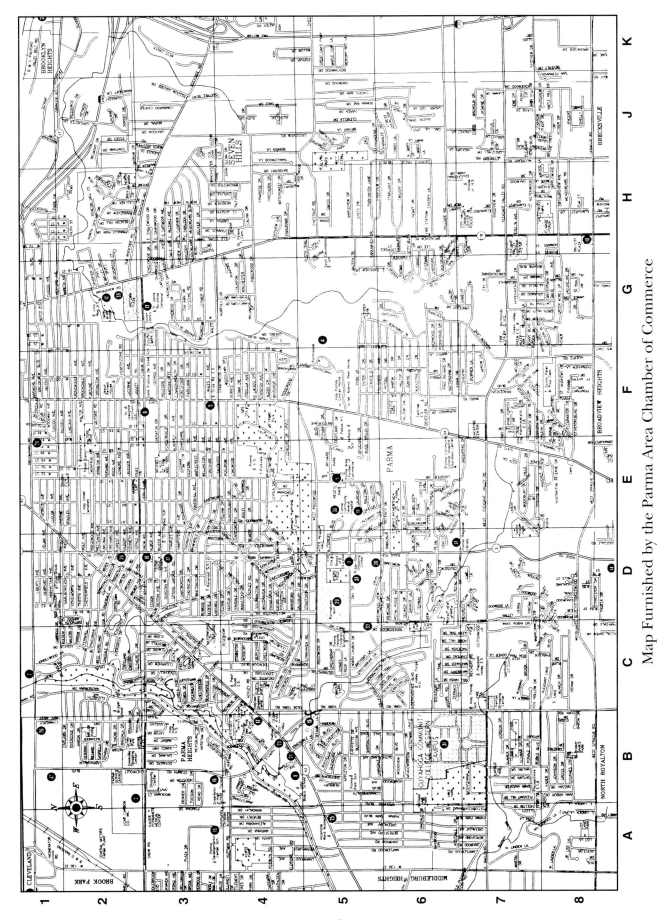

Map Furnished by the Parma Area Chamber of Commerce

TABLE OF CONTENTS

DEDICATED TO
GOD
FOR ALL HIS BLESSINGS ON OUR

CITY AND COUNTRY

IN ANTICIPATION OF
PARMA'S
175th ANNIVERSARY
AS A TOWNSHIP
IN 2001
AND
75th ANNIVERSARY
AS AN INCORPORATED TOWN
IN 1999

OUR COUNTRY'S
225th ANNIVERSARY
IN THE YEAR 2001

200th ANNIVERSARY OF
THE STATE OF OHIO IN
THE YEAR 2003

Psalm 127

"If the Lord does not build the house,
in vain do its builders labor;
if the lord does not watch over the city

in vain does the watchman keep vigil.

In vain is your earlier rising,
your going later to rest,
you who toil for the bread you eat
when he pours gifts on his beloved while they slumber"

INTRODUCTION

I know a man who bought land in Florida, and without knowing it, he found himself living on Sapsucker Lane. Though the bird is a beautiful bird, the name leaves a lot to be desired. How many of us check out the name of the street before we buy a house? Not many of us, I am sure, since it may not seem that important. However, it might be one of those deciding factors. It might be wise to do, so you do not end up on Sapsucker Lane!

Street names tell us many things about our community – its growth, its people, what they liked, their music, the shows they liked and many other social, religious and political aspects of their lives.

This study is not so much about music, or political or social developments, as it is about the people behind these developments; about those who gave us these street names and the reasons for giving us these names.

In this study we will deal with landowners, developers and just ordinary citizens who happened to become involved, in some way, with the history of our streets.

Each street has a dedication date, the earliest dedication date that could be found. This gives one the feeling of twentieth century development in Parma. For lack of a more practical reason, it gives residents on a street a reason to celebrate– like having a street party or maybe a street garage sale or some other quaint idea for celebrating. How about a street birthday cake at a street party? In any case, we hope you will enjoy the information herein. Research on this material was very interesting and challenging. There were difficulties in some of the spellings of names, dates of dedication of streets and contradictory reports on whom the streets were named after. However, most of these problems have been resolved. When there *is* some question on these matters, it is clearly stated. Interesting situations may arise: you may find, for example, that your house has been on your street long before the street was there. (Up until the time of dedication the street might have been a private road or not officially dedicated.) The dates of dedications were given to give you some idea as to when your neighborhood was changed from a woods, farm or wilderness into a community of friends and neighbors. Some streets have a number of dedication dates. As previously mentioned, we have provided the earliest possible dedication date for each street.

It is very difficult to know, sometimes, exactly what the developer had in mind when naming his street, especially when those who should know (relatives or co-workers) do not know. In some cases, historical records, for instance, (see Dorothy Avenue) suggest strongly the reason the street was named the way it was. When statements are made which are reasonable conjectures, this is clearly indicated. In fact, you may even have the opportunity to draw your own conclusions on two or three possibilities!

When our research yielded contradictory reports on whom the street was named after, these were always thoroughly examined, and the most plausible answer (along with the other possibilities) will be stated. Sometimes research will turn up answers that seem unlikely, but no other explanation is available. In these cases, the unlikely conclusion will be presented.

Aesthetically named streets which were clearly named for aesthetic reasons were touched on lightly. This is especially true when no one presently living could be found who knew why a street was called as it was. Some of these streets would require a study in the genealogy of the family to locate descendants. Close to 99% of those descendants contacted knew nothing about the naming of the street in question. To spend this kind of time on aesthetically named streets did not prove beneficial to the study.

To really understand the meaning of the dates of dedication of streets, it might help to get a few historical dates down to get the right perspective.

First of all, Brooklyn became a township in 1818. It included most of the near west side of Cleveland. The first meeting of what was to be the Rockport Township was held on February 24, 1819. On March 7, 1826, a new township was formed and it was called Parma Township. (The area was originally called Greenbriar.) On August 23, 1911, Parma Heights became a village, leaving the township government. Still Parma was not a village itself until December 15, 1924, when it was so incorporated. Many streets were dedicated before Parma was a village. It seems some of these dedications were handled by the county and others by the city of Cleveland. Parma became a city between 1920 and 1930. Most censuses would consider a city an incorporated village of 2,500 residents or more. Parma had 2,345 residents in 1920, and it was during the 1920's that the rural atmosphere began to disappear. In 1930 Parma had 13,890 residents. Thanks to Ernest Kubasek in his *History of Parma* and Dryck Bennett's book *On the Right Side of the Tracks and Between the Bridges* for the above dates.

All named streets of Parma are covered; however, there are a number of streets where definite information about the naming of the street could not be found. We have tried to present as much information as possible, supplemented by our own hypotheses.

Most of all, it is hoped that you will enjoy this book and, moreover, that no one will be offended by anything that is said within these pages. This report is based on careful research and seeks to present information positively and in a manner that will be appreciated by its readers.

There have been many interesting aspects to this study. First, there is the knowledge acquired through research about the detailed historical background of people in the community of Parma and those from outside of Parma who played a crucial role in the development of Parma as a community. Second, we learned about individuals who lived before us, ordinary people who never made the pages of history. It was very hard not to get lost in the lives of people who helped in the development of our community (which has been done on a few occasions). A book could be written on each of them. It was therefore necessary to limit our writings about individuals in order to completely address the intended subject.

The study of the naming of places and streets is in some way like studying ancient hieroglyphics (communication before written language on walls and stones). This study tells us things about people we would never have known, introducing us, in effect, to people we would have never met.

We learn about people and whom they loved. We learn about people and whom they feared. We learn that they had a sense of humor, a love of beauty, an appreciation of nature and many other things that we might not have known otherwise.

The nice thing about this study is that we learn about people right here in our own community. It is therefore hoped you will learn more about these wonderful people who helped make our community of Parma.

I have taken the liberty to give some personal impressions about some matters, but this is clearly indicated when such situations occur. This was done to give our friends outside our community a better understanding of our past and what we are like.

I want to make special mention of Ernest R. Kubasek's book *The History of Parma* and how much he and his book helped in this study.

_____

Streets and Roads . . . . You will find periodically in this book quotes about streets and roads, most of which have inspirational ideas. Hope you enjoy them. Where the publication is not mentioned the quote is taken from *The Home Book of Quotations* by Burton Stevenson.

Did you know . . . . Thanks to the University of Indiana Press and Larry L. Miller, author, for the use of material in their book *Ohio Place Names*, 1996.

INDEX FOR PICTURES

35. South Canterbury Road Home built in 1927.

36. Salisbury Drive Home built in 1926.

37. Salisbury Drive Home built in late 1920's.

38. Salisbury Drive Home built in late 1920's. Courtesy of Western Reserve Historical Society.

39. State Road looking north from State Road Hill. Grantwood is the first cross street. The Statewood Subdivision was started (left in lower part of picture). It was never developed and it eventually became Veterans' Park. (See Dellwood Drive for further information).

40. Top of this picture shows the homes being built in 1950's: Norris Avenue, Somia Drive, Priscilla Avenue, Dellwood Drive, Standish Avenue, Alden Avenue, Winthrop Drive, Ridgewood Drive (far to right) and Longwood Avenue (immediately to left). Also shown here is, just completed, Parma Senior High School.

41. Ridgewood Drive and Broadview Road in 1955. Notice the open area and lake south of Ridgewood Drive. In the open field north of Ridgewood Drive are where Staunton, Winchester, Yorktown, Williamsburg and Jamestown Drives are located now. Photographer was Robert Runyan from Collection of Bruce Young.

42. Marmore Avenue runs from State Road to West 33rd Street just south of Brookpark Road. Brookview Boulevard is second street south; Woodway Avenue and Freehold Avenue can be seen west of State Road. North Avenue and Tuxedo Avenue are located where the farm is on in this picture taken in 1949. Photographer was Robert Runyan from Collection of Bruce Young.

43. This picture shows Pearl Road, Ridge Road (lower left corner), Brookpark Road and train tracks. Other streets from Brookpark Road are: Velma Avenue, Luelda Avenue, Laverne Avenue and (bottom right) Maysday Avenue. Photographer was Robert Runyan, a Bruce Young Collection.

44. Byers Field in foreground; wooded area top of picture is where the Regency Apartments are now and where Regency Drive, Laurent Drive, Ralston Drive, Williston Drive, Lalemant Drive, Talbot Drive, Lynett Drive and Randolph Drive also located. Ridge Road is the two-lane road in front of the school building and notice Day Drive missing. Picture taken in 1955.

45. North of John Muir Elementary School; closest to the school is Brookdale Avenue, then Grovewood Avenue and Lincoln Avenue (top left of picture). Picture was taken 1950's. Street on left is West 24th Street. Notice the construction on Brookdale Avenue.

46. Notice South Park Boulevard (next to Quarry Creek, West Creek) top of picture (See South Park Boulevard for explanation). Other streets are Grantwood Drive, Wales Avenue, Wellington Avenue, Maplecrest Avenue, Parklane Drive, Heresford Drive. Photographer was Robert Runyan, a Bruce Young Collection. Photo taken in 1951.

47. This 1951 photograph shows the intersection of Brookpark and Broadview Roads. Also shown are Brookview Boulevard, North and Tuxedo Avenues. See also construction of Broadview/ Brookpark Shopping Center. Photographer was Robert Runyan, a Bruce Young Collection.

48. Sight of the first European settlement in Parma in 1816. Benajah Fay Family was the first family. The settlement was located (in this picture) at what now is the corner of Ridge Road and Theota Avenue. Bradley Avenue is one street north and Wolf Avenue is one street south. All were named after early settlers. One street south of Wolf Avenue is Ridgewood Avenue, which was the beginning of H. A. Stahl's work in Parma. Also shown is Maysday Avenue (lower right) and Kennilworth Avenue (upper right). Picture taken in 1948. Photographer was Robert Runyan from the Collection of Bruce Young.

49.   Streets from right are Grantwood Drive, Wales Avenue and Wellington Avenue. The school is State Road.

50.   You will notice behind Pleasant Valley Junior High School the construction on the home on West 101st Street (Dell Haven Drive), West 99th Street (Mayberry Drive), West 98th Street (Whitaker Drive) and West 96th Street (Chateau Drive). All the above numbered streets were changed to their names on June 26, 1962, in Ordinance 79-62. Reichert Road is also in the picture (east-west road). Picture taken in the late 1950's. Other streets in this development were West 92nd Street (Nobb Hill Drive), West 91st Street (Glenn Oval Drive) and West 94th Street (Hacienda Drive).

51.   Brookpark Road and Ridge Road intersection (top center looking North). Streets off Ridge Road, south of Brookpark Road, are: Liberty Avenue, Newport Avenue, Manhattan Avenue. Other side of the school is Marlborough Avenue and Kenilworth Avenue. The school is Ridge-Brook Elementary School. Picture taken in early 1950's.

52.   Streets in top half of picture are (from right): Theota Avenue (under construction), Lincoln Avenue, Russell Avenue; parts of Tuxedo Avenue visible. Picture taken in early 1950's. School is Thoreau Park Elementary School.

53.   Parma Greenbriar Estates were built in the late 1930's. Notice Snow Road and Big Creek Parkway; Hauserman Road (bottom right) with Brainard and Windham Drives going off Hauserman Road at Bottom right of picture. See Parkland Drive for information on this unique community. Photograph taken in 1930's.

NOTE:

*Special thanks to Superintendent Marsha Harrison
and the Parma City School District
for permission to use school pictures in this publication.*

LIST OF ILLUSTRATIONS

THE GARDEN CITY

The Garden City concept was originated in England by Sir Ebenezer Howard (1850-1928) in the late 1800's and early 1900's. He developed the idea that the Garden Cities of tomorrow would be cities which would maintain their populations at or below 30,000 citizens, have green parks, comfortable homes, and recreation centers. These cities would set standards of living that would be comfortable, peaceful and quiet with plenty of recreation facilities, including golf courses.

The first city set up on this order was Letchworth in the county of Hertfordshire, England, in 1903. In 1920 the town of Welwyn Garden City was founded, also in Hertfordshire. They called them the path to true reform, and truly they were. These Garden Cities influenced development throughout Europe and the United States. It seemed as if every country came up with its Garden City plans. They were preplanned areas ranging from private suburban developments to whole cities built with public funds.

Shaker Heights was developed with this Garden City philosophy in mind, and might not Parma also be part of this world-wide Garden City development in the early 1920's? We feel that Parma was truly part of this Garden City development. In the examination of our streets and their naming, we hope to show you why we feel this is so.

Howard A. Stahl

HOWARD A. STAHL, A TRIBUTE

A man, little known and almost a stranger in the Parma community, had, whether we know it or not, quite an influence on our lives. He was a man of exceptional talents and accomplishments. He affected the lives of over a half million people in the last 75 years, not only here in Parma but also in communities like Lakeland, Florida, where he had a multimillion dollar development in the 1920's. In North Madison, Ohio, he also had another multi-million dollar development. He was a real-estate developer in Parma in the 1920's and laid out Parma Circle, which, it appears, he intended to develop into an exclusive community of upper class residential homes. This area extends from West 54th Street to Westminster Drive, from south of Parmatown to just short of Snow Road. (See picture, page 24, and plat maps, pages 22 and 23.) He purchased the land and laid out an extensive street plan for the township and village. From his plans it appears he wanted to make it into a Garden City in a manner similar to Shaker Heights, which was a Garden City. The early homes that were built were large brick and frame homes similar to what you might see in Shaker Heights today. (See pictures starting on page 23.) His plans also included a golf course (Ridgewood Country Club), lakes, parks, and winding roads, typical again of a Garden City community. All this work of Mr. Stahl was done in the 1920's. His offices were in the Hitchcock Building in downtown Cleveland and at Cedar and Coventry Roads in Cleveland Heights. He and his wife lived on South Woodland Road in Shaker Heights, Ohio.

The streets in Shaker Heights were laid out from 1910 to 1925 by the Van Sweringen brothers and the F. A. Pease Engineering Company, which worked closely with the brothers. Harry Gallimore, who was an engineer for the Pease Company, and who served for many years as city engineer for Shaker Heights, was an avid reader of English literature. It seems that in London, England, at the time, developers were creating suburban towns for the wealthy, where those who could afford it could live in quiet luxury when they returned to their homes from the smoke-filled industrial cities. They were called Garden Cities, and the names given the streets and communities were classic English names. When the Van Sweringens heard of these Garden Cities, they wanted to incorporate a similar idea into their town. Some reports say they went so far as to get a postal directory from England to get the names of the streets and cities for their new community. The result is what we have in Shaker Heights today and even in Parma! Yes, the Van Sweringen brothers had an office on Coventry, just a short distance from Howard A. Stahl's office. H. A. Stahl was considered a major developer in his day, and it is most likely that the Van Sweringens and Stahl were acquainted. The Van Sweringen brothers had great plans for Shaker Heights. Many of the names for the streets in Parma were taken from Shaker Heights or from the same English sources, an English postal directory and the names of English towns.

Stahl's Garden community of "Cleveland Heights" (the name he gave it) in Lakeland, Florida, is an outstanding example of his vision: an ideal community of upper middle class to upper class living (see plat map, page 26). It was a community of beautiful property sights with parks, playgrounds, lakes and a golf course of 6,302 yards (see pictures on page 27). The Cleveland Heights of Lakeland, Florida, consisted of 1080 home sites with 32 streets and 150 acres devoted to the golf course. It was well planned with all aspects of living considered. The city park around the beautiful Hollingsworth Lake was circled by Hollingsworth Road, with large homes facing the lake from the other side of Hollingsworth Road. The park around the lake consisted of five acres. If you were a property owner anywhere in the Cleveland Heights community, you were a member of the country club and could use all the recreation facilities. Mr. and Mrs. Harrison Gleason, friends of the Stahls, said they had some wonderful times together at the Cleveland

H. A. STAHL'S

RIDGEWOOD DEVELOPMENT

1920 TO 1930

GARDEN CITY

OF

PARMA

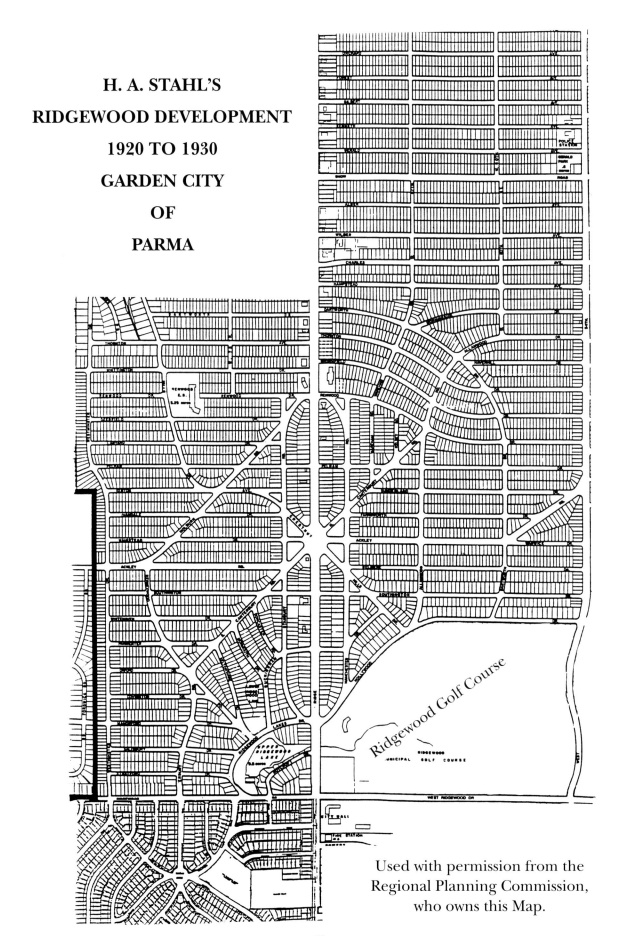

Ridgewood Golf Course

Used with permission from the
Regional Planning Commission,
who owns this Map.

RIDGEWOOD SUBDIVISION NO.11 (1926)
Parmatown Mall Now

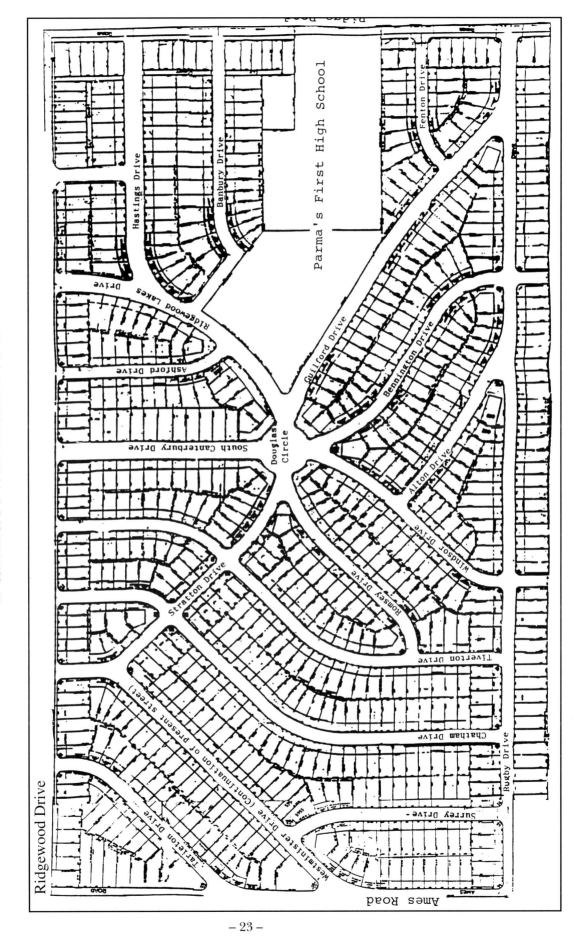

2

This is a 1927 picture of Parma's Ridgewood Circle. A Development of H. A. Stahl.
Picture courtesy of Western Reserve Historical Society.

Heights center in Florida. Mr. Stahl would be proud of Cleveland Heights today, as the community has continued to epitomize Mr. Stahl's vision of distinction and refinement with its beautiful home sites and parks in a casual setting. (See Plat Map on page 26.)

A statement on a brochure for the Cleveland Heights Country Club in Florida gives a good picture of Mr. Stahl's intentions in Parma:

> *"The H. A. Stahl Properties Co. established at Cleveland in 1912, is an experienced and financially responsible corporation, which has successfully created, developed and operated several high-class residential and country club properties. Madison Golf Lakelands, on Lake Erie near Cleveland with two golf courses, half a mile of beach, a magnificent clubhouse, tennis and roque courts, riding stables, etc., is nationally known for its high grade character and excellence. The Stahl Company also owns Ridgewood, a new home and recreational development in Cleveland, covering 1,250 acres with playgrounds, lakes, an eighteen hole golf course and every modern improvement. Over two-thirds of Ridgewood's 7,000 lots were already sold."*

Stahl's garden summer resort of North Madison, Ohio, which opened in 1923, consisted of many summer homes on long beautiful streets engulfed by large trees; some say he must have spent thousands of dollars on those beautiful trees. Every street is lined with these large trees that give an arch-like appearance and plenty of shade in the summertime (in a time before air conditioning). Stahl called it his summer colony. This resort was for the wealthy of Northwest Pennsylvania and Northeast Ohio. Summer homes were built on these long beautiful streets (see Plat Map, page 28, and pictures, page 29). He had a beautiful country club where an eight-piece orchestra played every Saturday night in his screened-in ballroom during the summer months. There were tennis courts and sandy beaches on the Lake Erie shore line and many other recreational activities. In an advertisement we read:

> *"Madison Golf Lakeland is an institution. It was conceived and created as a summer home of refinement, distinction and high ideals."*

H. A. Stahl and his wife, Agnes, had a summer home on Lake Erie at the North Madison resort (see picture 12, page 30). Stahl sold the golf course to the property owners in 1925.

Stahl's Garden community of Parma, of which Ridgewood Country Club was a part, gives us a good idea what he had in mind. We quote from the original brochure of H. A. Stahl's Ridgewood Country Club:

> *"Every modern feature was incorporated in the laying out of creeping bent greens of velvety texture. The scenic beauty of Ridgewood is simply marvelous due to the hilly character of the land and magnificent trees and flowering shrubs which were left to remain in their native splendor."*

He had plans for recreational facilities, churches and playgrounds but no commercial area since this was not part of the Garden City philosophy.

His Garden City of Parma was in its infant stage when the Depression hit him and hit him hard. He had all the streets dedicated and many improvements in. He was working closely with the new city government (Parma became a village in December 1924) in planning an outstanding community. Ernest Kubasek in his *History of Parma* says:

COMMUNITY OF CLEVELAND HEIGHTS

A Highly Restricted Residence

Golf & Country Club Development at Lakeland, Florida

AND

OWNED AND DEVELOPED BY

THE H.A. STAHL
FLORIDA PROPERTIES COMPANY

108 S. TENNESSEE AVE.   LAKELAND, FLA.

ST. PETERSBURG OFFICE .... 532-534 CENTRAL AVE.
TAMPA OFFICE .... CRESCENT APTS., LAFAYETTE ST., WEST
CLEVELAND OFFICE .... HICKOX BUILDING

T. B. BROWN .... Sales Director
G. T. WHITMORE, JR. .... Sales Director
CAPT. J. H. REDING .... Civil Engineer
A. D. TAYLOR .... Consulting Landscape Architect
C. E. SWINEHART .... Landscape Architect
H. P. WHITWORTH .... Architect
WM. S. FLYNN .... Golf Architect

N

LAKE HOLLINGSWORTH

SO. FLORIDA AVENUE

ENLARGED DETAIL OF BUSINESS DISTRICT.
Scale F. 100

Map Furnished by
Cleveland Heights Country Club
Lakeland, Florida

Cleveland Heights
Golf Course
Lakeland, Florida
(For explanation, see
"H. A. Stahl, A Tribute").

3

4 Cleveland Heights Community
Lakeland, Florida

5 Cleveland Heights Country Club
Lakeland, Florida

6 North Madison Country Club
(For explanation, see "H. A. Stahl, A Tribute").

7 North Madison Country Club
(Madison Golfland), North Madison, Ohio.

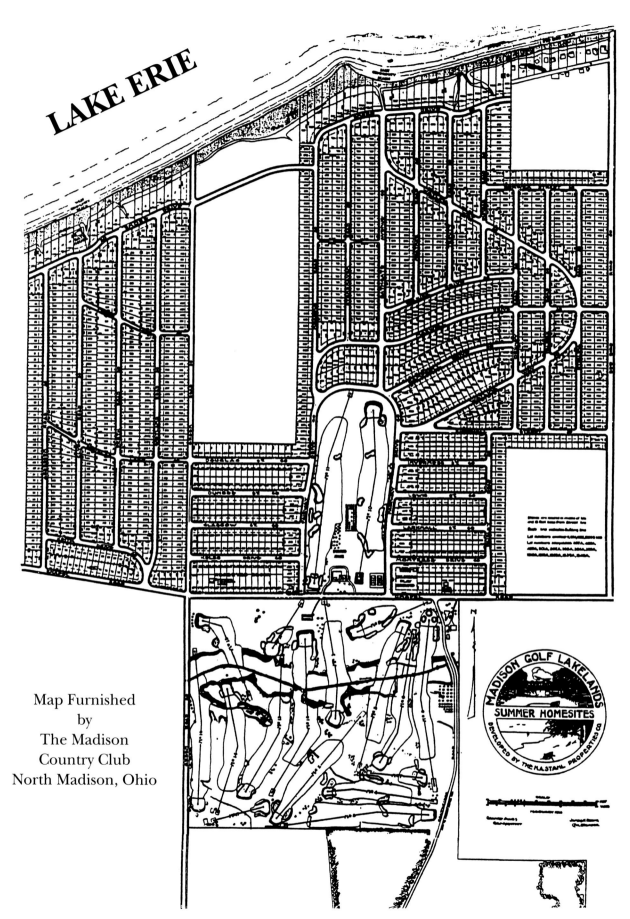

LAKE ERIE

Map Furnished
by
The Madison
Country Club
North Madison, Ohio

8

North Madison
H. A. Stahl's Development in 1920's

9

North Madison
H. A. Stahl's Development in 1920's

10

North Madison
H. A. Stahl's
Development
in 1920's

11

H. A. Stahl's Home
17200 South Woodland Road
Shaker Heights

H. A. Stahl's home
on Lake Erie,
North Madison, Ohio

12

Green Lake,
H. S. Stahl's backyard,
17200 South Woodland Road
Shaker Heights, Ohio

13

H. A. Stahl lost everything in the Depression and died a short time later of heart failure, but he set Parma on a course that led this community into a major building development that gave Parma the reputation as the fastest growing community in the country during the 1950's. The 1950's development was done on H. A. Stahl's streets. He was the first real developer in Parma and set the stage for other developers to try their hand in this new village of Cuyahoga County.

H. A. Stahl was born in 1875. He was the only child of Henry H. Stahl and Laura (Hale) Stahl. (Laura Stahl was related to the Hales of Hale's Farm and Village of the Western Reserve Historical Society.) Stahl's family settled in Ohio as early as 1807.

H. A. Stahl married Agnes Whitmore of Mogadore, Ohio, on September 10, 1907. According to Mr. and Mrs. Harrison Gleason, family friends and neighbors, the Stahls had no children. Probate court records also indicate this.

Howard and Agnes lived at 17200 South Woodland Road in Shaker Heights, Ohio. The house is a beautiful example of Dutch Colonial Revival with a gambrel roof. It was located on the corner of Attleboro and South Woodland Road and overlooked Green Lake, one of the famous Shaker Lakes (see pictures 11 and 13 on page 30).

What happened to H. A. Stahl (this is the way he signed all his legal papers) is not exactly clear. Some believed he worked for the county after he lost everything in the Depression and survived for a short time. He died on December 24, 1931, of heart failure. He was 56 years old.

According to court records, he was $111,964.88 in debt at the time of his death. (This amount includes claims of general creditors against him and also doctors' bills he incurred towards the end of his life.) His wife, Agnes, was permitted to keep their home in Shaker Heights, but she must have returned to her hometown in Mogadore, Ohio, as that is where she buried her husband.

Howard A. Stahl is a man long-forgotten; a man who did a lot for people in his time and for us today. He was wealthy, but he knew how to work. He also put a lot of his money back into the community. He worked for a better community for which we can be grateful today.

Because of the Depression, H. A. Stahl was never able to follow through on his plans for Parma. Others took on Stahl's idea and initiative, and we have, for instance, the Greenbriar Community, which was developed by A. F. Hamel, Fred Greiner and Frank D. Johnson in the early to late 1930's after Stahl's death. This community was organized similarly to Shaker Heights. The names of the streets were taken directly from Shaker Heights. (Examples include Elsmere Drive, Parkland Drive, Enderby Drive and Edgehill Drive). It was an exclusive community of large and expensive homes. In many ways this community was governed by the owners.

LAKELAND, FLORIDA, AND PARMA, OHIO, STREETS

SIMILAR STREET NAMES IN GARDEN COMMUNITIES

Lakeland, Florida	Parma, Ohio	Shaker Heights Cleveland Heights
Buckingham Avenue	Buckingham Drive	
Southington Avenue	Southington Drive	Southington Road
Stratford Lane	Stratford Drive	Stratford Road
Renwood Avenue	Renwood Drive	
Derbyshire Road		Derbyshire Road
Charles Street	Charles Avenue	
Ridgewood Street	Ridgewood Drive	
Coventry Avenue	Coventry Drive	Coventry Road
Fairmont Street		Fairmont Boulevard
Kensington Street		Kensington Road
Cambridge Avenue	Cambridge Drive	Cambridge Road
Kerneywood Street	Kerneywood Road	
Clearview Avenue	Clearview Avenue	
Woodward Street		Woodward Avenue
Sagamore Street	Sagamore Road	
Warrington Avenue		Warrington Road
Oxford Avenue	Oxford Drive	Oxford Road
Monticello Avenue		Monticello Boulevard
Kenilworth Place	Kenilworth Avenue	Kenilworth Road
Morningside Drive	Morningside Drive	
	Drexmore Drive	Drexmore Road
	Dartmoor Avenue	Dartmoor Road
	Malvern Avenue	Malvern Road
	Sedgewick Avenue	Sedgewick Road
	Norwood Avenue	Norwood Road
	Attleboro Avenue	Attleboro Road
	Canterbury Road	Canterbury Road
	Eaton Drive	Eaton Road
	Kenmore Avenue	Kenmore Road
	Glencairn Drive	Glencairn Road
	Elsmere Drive	Elsmere Road
	Enderby Drive	Enderby Road
	Onaway Oval	Onaway Road
	Parkland Drive	Parkland Drive
	South Park Boulevard	South Park Boulevard
	Ingleside Drive	Ingleside Road
	Kenyon Drive	Kenyon Road
	Keystone Road	Keystone Road
	Park Drive	Park Drive
	Torrington Avenue	Torrington Road

EARLY DEVELOPERS

A MAN WITH A PLAN

Don Helwick was a developer who built homes east of West 54th Street up to and including the Quarry Creek area. He had great plans for Parma, planning to use the Quarry Creek area as a beautiful park with winding boulevards around it and beautiful homes in and around this park. He wanted homes for both the wealthy and middle-income families. Many of his street names were taken from those of Cleveland Heights or Shaker Heights. Interestingly enough, he planned South Park Boulevard on the west side of Quarry Creek and South Park Boulevard East (now Ravine Boulevard) on the east side of Quarry Creek. The name seems to have been taken directly from Shaker Heights since South in Parma's South Park Boulevard has little meaning since the street runs on the west side of the proposed park, not south. It seems that he had ideas of the Garden City development. The streets' names and the community design indicate this. He named one street Sedgewick, the name (Sedgewick Land Company) given to the syndicate set up by the Van Sweringen brothers to develop the Garden city of Shaker Heights (see Sedgewick Avenue for more information). Also, could the name HelWICK have something to do with the name SedgeWICK? We might never know. Don Helwick lost everything in the Depression – a real tragedy for the family. He lived on Overlook Road (another street name in Parma) in Cleveland Heights. The Helwicks had four children. Mr. Helwick died in 1935. For more information, see "Quarry Creek: The Forgotten Tributary." (See pictures 26 and 46.)

KLEIN-LAMPL OPENS BROADVIEW DOOR

Another developer in Parma in the 1920's was Jack Lampl, who worked mainly in the Broadview-Brookpark area. He lived on Orville Avenue in Glenville near University Circle in Cleveland. The company was called the Klein-Lampl Home Sites. This company set up Parkleigh Drive, Meadowlawn Boulevard, Dartmoor Drive, Clearview Avenue and Hillside Avenue. These streets were all dedicated in the years 1926-1927, but few homes were built.

Herman Klein, partner in the Klein-Lampl Company, was also a developer in Miami, Florida. The Miami communities were Waterberry, Riveria Park and Coral Way Center. Herman Klein lived in the Cleveland Heights - Shaker Heights area.

QUARRY CREEK:
THE FORGOTTEN TRIBUTARY *

Little known, and little appreciated, Quarry Creek still stands as a natural landmark in the Parma area. During our research on the streets of Parma, the Historical Society secured a report from the Cuyahoga River Community Planning Organization (CRCPO) on the history and evaluation of Quarry Creek. Quarry Creek runs from Biscayne Boulevard, located in the southern hills of Parma, and passes through many residential areas, creating storybook sights as it goes. It winds through a deep wooded ravine past the Henninger Home, which at one time overlooked it from its hillside location, through Brooklyn Heights into the Cuyahoga River.

In the history of the Quarry Creek, which has been called West Creek, Glen Creek and South Park Creek, there were three attempts to build this outstanding nature area into a park. Two attempts took place in the early 1900's. Both failed. In 1919 the Board of Park Commissioners attempted to purchase this "Story Book land" as part of the Cleveland Metropolitan Park System. However, the residents and the Park Board could not come to terms. The Park Board was still willing to negotiate. It was during this time (1920's) that Don Helwick planned and set up roads and homesites around this beautiful "park." He set up South Park Boulevard on the west side of the "park" and South Park Boulevard East (now Ravine Boulevard) on the east side of the "park." It appeared that both streets were to follow Quarry Creek, winding through the woods to Wick Road (Grantwood Drive) or Ridgewood Drive. Mr. Helwick had some great plans for this community. The names of the streets were classic English names, and he wanted both the wealthy and ordinary citizen to enjoy the area since he had plans for large homes and middle-income homes. This area would be centered around Quarry Creek as a natural park. (Much of this is considered in detail in the history of the streets section; see Keystone Road, South Park Boulevard and other streets.) It seems he planned to have a park made of Quarry Creek and possibly turn it over to the Township or to Cleveland Metropolitan Parks. That never happened. Mr. Helwick lost everything in the Depression. It was a real tragedy for the Helwick Family and for Parma.

The third attempt to save this outstanding area was made by the West Creek preservation committee in 1998 headed by David J. Vasarhelyi. They attempted to get a levy passed by the voters to save this land for the Parma citizens. The issue, which was known as issue 22, failed.

Laura McShane of CRCPO did a study of Quarry Creek in 1994, and it is worth quoting from it: "Hiking this creek from Ridgewood Drive in Parma, one encounters high shale walls not unlike the cliffs found along the Rocky River in the Cleveland Metroparks Reservation. Between Grantwood Drive and Snow Road the creek forms a steep ravine.... The creek cascades along suburban South Park Boulevard carving through the sand stone and shale to form wet rock cliffs and rock shelves draped with vines and moss. This is a children's world of make-believe forts and narrow outlaw trails along the slopes . . . . This park looks and feels like a Cleveland Metropark with its wooded hillsides and steep shale cliffs bordering the river. It is ironic that Quarry Creek, which has much of the same characteristics of the other streams preserved within the Cleveland Metroparks, remains largely unnoticed. . . . it (finally) merges anonymously with the Cuyahoga River and flows onward to Lake Erie. Quarry Creek did not make it into the System."

In talking with a few residents who live on Quarry Creek, we got a very good response. Mrs. Margaret (Donahoe) Miktuk, who lives next to the creek on Ridgewood Drive (their sun deck overlooks the creek behind their home; see picture 18), says they enjoy sitting on their deck watching the water passing their home and just listening to the water after a heavy rain. They also walk up the creek into the woods.

Frances Dasko, who lives next to the creek on Grantwood Drive, says she loves the scenery and the animals. It feels, from her deck, as if she were lost in the woods. The plans for her home refer to Quarry Creek as South Park Creek. Her home was built in 1957 and is right on the cliff overlooking Quarry Creek.

One family on Ridgewood Drive has Quarry Creek passing right through its front yard, at which point the creek is about 15 feet wide. During rainy times of year, the water is a sight to behold.

These are only a few of the stories of Quarry Creek that might make us appreciate even more the great natural heritage that Parma has. One can truly appreciate also the attempts by the Park System, and by Don Helwick, the developer, and by West Creek Preservation Committee to save this area for a park.

––––––––––––

Thanks to Laura McShane and the Cuyahoga River Community Planning Organization (CRCPO) for this title and for their report.

STREET NAMES REFLECT
THE THINKING OF THE COMMUNITY

We have records of streets that at one time existed but either had their names changed to street numbers or were eliminated completely. One of these streets is Bellman Road. It had its name changed to Windermere Road in 1932 (Windermere is a town in Northern England in Cambria County) and now neither street is in existence. Another change in 1932 was that Dartmoor Avenue was changed to Drexmore Avenue because Dartmoor was confused with Dartworth Drive. (There are a Drexmore Road in Shaker Heights and a Dartmoor Road in Cleveland Heights.) The surviving name now is Dartmoor, so either it was not changed as indicated by the Ordinance or neither of the above streets is in existence now. It is believed that the present Dartmoor is a different street altogether. We lost the streets of Jermain and Bakely Avenues. Malverne and Sedgewick Avenues gave way to numbered streets West 33rd and West 29th, respectively. (See these entries in the streets section.) In 1932 there were many streets that lost their names to numbers. Apparently, the city thought it was more important to use the streets for locating house numbers. Thorman Avenue was changed to West 78th Street. Beech Avenue was changed to West 94th Street. West State Alley was changed to West 37th Street, and East Alley was changed to West 35th Street. Homewood Avenue was changed to West 119th Street, and Norwood Avenue (there is a Norwood Road in Shaker Heights) was changed to West 118th Street. Attleboro Avenue (the name of the street in Shaker Heights where Mr. H. A. Stahl lived) was changed to West 116th Street. Southerland Avenue was changed to West 115th street. Fairfax Avenue was changed to West 114th Street. Creighton Avenue was changed to West 112th Street. Rosedale was changed to West 111th Street. Lockwood Avenue was changed to West 109th Street. Akin Avenue was changed to West 108th Street. Cross Street was changed to West 24th Street.

Thirty years later, in 1962, the feeling was just the opposite. There was a mass movement to change numbered streets to named streets when West 91st, 92nd, 94th, 96th, 98th, 99th, and 101st were to changed to Glen Oval, Nobb Hill, Hacienda, Chateau, Whitaker, Mayberry, and Dell Haven Drives, respectively. In the Pleasant Valley Road area West 116th, 118th, 119th, 121st, 122nd and 123rd Streets were changed to Malibu, Skylark, Dawn Haven, Nassau, Ann Arbor, Pleasant Hill and Sleepy Hollow Drives.

More recently, on March 18, 1996, West 58th was changed to Brittany Drive by council at the request of Councilman Paul Kirner, who requested it be named after his godchild, Brittany Kelley.

The above shows how the naming of the streets reflects the people's thinking during these periods of history.

STREETS

AND

THEIR

NAMES

STREETS OF PARMA, HOW THEY WERE NAMED
AND OTHER HISTORIC INFORMATION

AARON DRIVE (B2)

Aaron Drive was dedicated on January 18, 1954. This street was named after Aaron Miller, Sam Miller's oldest son, who was born on March 25, 1949. Sam Miller was the developer for Forest City Enterprises. (Information from Vol. 7711, page 520, County Plat Books and Sam Miller himself.)

ABBOT DRIVE (F6)

Abbot Drive was dedicated on April 18, 1966. It was part of the Richard Subdivision #8 (City Ordinance 151-66). The word "Abbot" is the name of a man who is superior of an abbey for men. It is not clear why this street was named as such. The street, however, is located in the area of the so-called "Robinhood Estates," which might account for the name Abbot. It is interesting how this street was arranged. You have to go through the Abbot (Abbot Drive) to get to the King (King Richard Drive). There is no other way. (See King Richard Drive for further information.)

ABRAHAM DRIVE (B2)

Abraham Drive was dedicated on September 27, 1954, in Ordinance 198-54 by Parma City Council at the request of Sunrise Development. Sam Miller was the developer for Forest City. This street was named after one of Sam Miller's sons, Abraham Miller. (Information from Sam Miller himself.)

ACKLEY ROAD (D4)

Ackley Road was dedicated (in Parma) on June 28, 1922 (County plat Ridgewood Estates #5). It was named after the Ackley family, who owned land at the (now) Old York Road and Pearl Road

intersection (Northwest Section) located in Parma Heights. The street, however, was carried on into Parma. In 1903, Lottie L. Ackley owned the land where the street originates today. The street now extends through Parma Circle and terminates at West 54th Street.

ADKINS WAY (D8)

This street was originally dedicated as Woodlands Boulevard on June 15, 1992, in Ordinance 63-92. However, the residents requested the name be changed to Adkins Way. City Council changed the name on October 6, 1997. Adkins Way leads into the Pine Tree Estates north off Sprague Road. Dennis Adkins, the man for whom this street was named, died October 1, 1996, at the age of 61 while helping one of his neighbors. It seems he was known for helping his neighbors, especially when his help was needed. It was the "Adkins' Way." He retired from General Motors after 35 years and spent his time helping people. It was one year after his death that the neighbors had this street named in his honor.

ALBER AVENUE (D3)

This street has an interesting history. "George Alber (1870-1945) tried his fortunes in many ways and finally became a carpenter and builder of homes in the Cleveland area." The Alber family lived on Holmden Avenue in Cleveland. He did start building in Rocky River and the West Park of Cleveland (there is a street in Cleveland named Alber Avenue), and it is believed he is responsible for setting up Alber Avenue in Parma. However, for some reason, he never built homes here in Parma. Like many builders at the time, he lost everything in the Depression, or perhaps H. A. Stahl could have bought him out. The street was dedicated on December 22, 1922. (Information is from Gary Alber, George's son, on July 25, 1989.) The first sentence above was quoted by Gary Alber from the family history. Even though this was an H. A. Stahl development (Ridgewood Garden Annex No. 2), it is believed that George Alber played a major part in the development of this street.

ALBERTLY AVENUE (E3)

This street was dedicated originally in two parts. The original dedication, near State Road, was on September 18, 1920, and recorded on December 17, 1920 (County plat Map Vol. 71 page 13). Joshua Bingham, president of the Bingham-Priest Company, named the street. The development was called the Romona Heights Subdivision. The extension, near West 54th Street, was dedicated on November 8, 1922. There is no immediate indication why they picked the name Albertly. All presently known sources of research have been investigated, but no conclusive answer has been obtained. Some even felt it might have had something to do with Alber Avenue, dedicated on December 22, 1922, a street just across West 54th Street from Albertly Avenue. There is no evidence to prove this either. Then again we have Wilber Avenue, dedicated on December 22, 1922, in the same area, but this street itself is a puzzle. Research still continues.

ALDEN DRIVE (F4)

This street is thought to have been named after John Alden of the early Pilgrims. It seems the early settlers, the Snow family (for which Snow Road is named), were descendants of the Pilgrims (a genealogy is on file at the Historical Society). This street was named when the Snow family still had influence in the area. According to the genealogy, the Snows were the direct descendants of John Alden. This street was dedicated on June 6, 1955 (ordinance 124-55) at the request of the Mayflower Development Company. No member of the Snow family worked for the Mayflower Development that we

know. This could not be verified even by the Snow Family descendants or by someone who knows of them, but the above information would indicate that there is a strong possibility that this street got its name from the Snow family or friends of the Snow family. The real estate company involved was Puritan Realty. The other streets in the area named after the Pilgrims were Standish Avenue (Captain Miles Standish), Priscilla Avenue, (Priscilla Mullins), and Winthrop Drive; hence the above conclusion. Alden and Mullins are also mentioned in Longfellow's *The Courtship of Miles Standish.* (See picture 40.)

ALEXANDER DRIVE (B2)

Alexander Drive is probably named after a man or child of a man involved in the development of this subdivision as many of the streets of this subdivision were. But this could not be verified. This street is called Avenue in court records but everywhere else it is called Drive. Mrs. Frank Ference, who lives on the street, says that it has been known both as Drive and Avenue, and she wasn't sure which was the correct name. She said she likes Drive because Avenue gives the impression of being a broad street and Alexander is a quiet small residential street. She says she really likes her street. It is quiet at night and there is a park nearby. Alexander Drive was originally dedicated on January 18, 1954 (Vol. 7711, page 520 County Plat Books). Other streets in this area were given names taken from Biblical times. However, some of the names were also names of children of the developers. At this time there is no definite answer to the naming of this street. Research is still being carried on. Another date of dedication was given at city hall as June 20, 1955, in Ordinance 144-55.

ALLANWOOD ROAD (E4)

This street was dedicated on June 15, 1921 (County Plat Books Vol. 80, page 32). It is officially spelled Allanwood. This street is part of the H. A. Stahl Development. It appears H. A. Stahl applied many of the ideas in Parma that were used in setting up Shaker Heights; namely, he followed the Garden City philosophy. They used the winding roads, lakes, and a golf course. The street names were taken from Shaker Heights streets or taken from the same English source from which the Shaker Heights streets were named, the Garden Cities of England in the 1920's. H. A. Stahl lived in Shaker Heights in the 1920's and had an office at Cedar and Coventry Roads. Research has not uncovered any reason for this street being named as it is except that it is an aesthetically appealing name from the Garden City source. It is interesting to note that there is a street by this name in Lakeland, Florida, in the area where H. A. Stahl developed a subdivision called the "Cleveland Heights Subdivision." (See in this book "H. A. Stahl, A Tribute" for further information.)

AMBER LANE (C7)

Amber Lane was dedicated on July 7, 1980, (Ordinance 114-79) at the request of the Sunrise Development Company and is part of Black Forest Acres. The word "amber" is generally known as a descriptive word for something with a yellowish-brown color. The choice of name may have had something to do with the Sunrise Builders (above) in following through with their theme for the development. Amber Lane is a north-south street off Fox Hollow Drive, which runs off York Road, south of Pleasant Valley.

AMES ROAD (C7)

This street was dedicated on May 4, 1959 (City Ordinance 83-59). This street is part of the H. A. Stahl Development, even though this street was dedicated some 26 years after H. A. Stahl's death. This is part of what Mr. Stahl had in mind for a residential development for the Parmatown area called Ridgewood Subdivision 11 (see page 23 and 24). Ames Drive is the only surviving street in his layout of the Parmatown Area. The reason why it was dedicated so many years later is because H. A. Stahl lost everything in the Depression and could not complete his

plans. When Parmatown was set up, the city used the same name for this street that he had in his plans for residential development. His plans, it seems, were to continue the Garden City concept in this development. It might be interesting to note that there is a town in England called Amesbury. (See in this book "H. A. Stahl, A Tribute" for more information.)

AMHERST DRIVE (D2)

Amherst Drive was dedicated on November 6, 1961, in Ordinance 200-61. It is part of the Fernhill Heights development. It would appear that this street was named after Amherst College in Amherst, Massachusetts. The reason for this assumption is that all the streets in this development were named after small elite institutions of learning. Amherst College has an enrollment of 1,570 students. Homes on one side of Amherst Drive back up to a city park which gives the residents open spaces. It might be noted also that Daniel Smith, for whom Smith Road was named, was from Amherst, Massachusetts. In 1832 he had a 100-acre farm at what is now Smith and Pearl Roads. (Information is from *History of Brookpark* by W. F. Holzworth.)

ANDOVER DRIVE (E8)

This street was developed by Lee Gettling and Richard Needles and was dedicated on February 21, 1989, in Ordinance 47-89. The builder did not give a reason that could be verified for naming this street the way he did; however, there is a little town in Northeast Ohio near Pymatuning Lake, a recreation center, called Andover. Since the other streets in this community were also named after recreation areas, this might be the reason for naming this street Andover. Pymatuning Lake and this city are quite popular.

ANN ARBOR DRIVE (B7)

This street was originally called West 121st Street and was dedicated on February 4, 1957. On

September 4, 1962, in Ordinance 104-62, the name was changed by City Council at the request of the residents to Ann Arbor Drive. Residents of 1962 who still live on Ann Arbor Drive could give no reason for picking the Ann Arbor name. Ann Arbor is a city in Michigan where the University of Michigan is located.

ANTOINETTE DRIVE (E6)

Antoinette Drive was originally dedicated on December 17, 1979, in city Ordinance 190-79. Later, another part was dedicated on January 7, 1988, as part of the Ridge Vista Estates. The developer, who used French names for his streets, states that this street was given this name because of its aesthetic sound. He would give no other reason for naming this street. The historic Marie Antoinette (1755-1793) was married to Louis XVI of France and was the daughter of Maria Theresa of Austria.

APOLLO DRIVE (B7)

Apollo Drive was originally dedicated as West 111th Street on May 5, 1958, in Ordinance 124-58. It was changed to Apollo Drive on July 1, 1963, in Ordinance 148-63. This street was probably named after NASA's Apollo program which was in full swing at the time, even though the Apollo mission has not yet come to fruition. This hypothesis, however, could not be verified. Note of interest: Apollo was the name of the mythological god of song and poetry. It is a little complicated but the phrase "Swan Song" comes from this ancient pagan god Apollo. The ancients believed the swan would burst into song upon its approaching death as it was going to meet its god Apollo; thus the last work of a writer or orator is called his or her "Swan Song." (Information is from *Hog on Ice* by Charles Funk.)

ARBOR DRIVE (C7)

The word "arbor" means tree, and this street is located among a group of aesthetically named thoroughfares. It was dedicated on October 9, 1968 (Vol. 218 page 41A County Plat Maps), at the request of the K & F Builders as Northern Ohio Subdivision #1. City Hall had a dedication date of January 3, 1977, in city Ordinance 220-76. Arbor Drive is located among streets that wind around a hilly countryside, giving a pleasant appearance.

ARCADIA DRIVE (D6)

This street was dedicated on July 2, 1957 (Ordinance number 195-57). Seltzer-Wickman-Stormes were the developers. Arcadia refers to a region or scene of simple pleasure or quiet. An Arcadian is a person who lives a simple life. Arcadia is also a region of ancient Greece. We infer that one of the above is the source of this street's name.

ARDEN ROAD (D2)

This street was laid out by the Wooster Parkway Company, of which W. L. Douglas was president and H. A. Stahl was secretary. Owners of the land were William Wolf, Laura Wolf and James Bingham. This street was dedicated on December 18, 1919 (Vol. 67 page 9). Extensive research has not uncovered the reason for this street being named Arden. There was a revolutionary patriot named Jacob Arden who was involved in many demonstrations against the British and eventually joined the Army in the Revolutionary War. He eventually died in the war. It seems possible that someone might have been related to him from New York. (There were many settlers in Parma from New York, where this patriot was well known.) There are, moreover, several places in England that have this name which might have influenced the naming of this street. This is the first appearance of H. A. Stahl in Parma. He laid out much of Parma. It is interesting to note that a street in Lakeland, Florida, where H. A. Stahl set up a large development (the "Cleveland Heights area") has a street named Arden. (See "H. A. Stahl: A Tribute" in this book.)

ARROW LANE (F7)

This street was dedicated on March 9, 1964, in Parma City Ordinance 52-64. It is one of the streets in the Robinhood development which included such street names as Bowman Lane, Robinhood Drive, King Richard Drive, Sherwood Drive, Nottingham Drive and Friar Drive. It would seem that Arrow Lane is in good company with the above names. This was a Gulfedge Subdivision.

ARROWWOOD OVAL (D7)

This street was dedicated on December 7, 1970, in Ordinance number 352-70. It appears to be an aesthetically named street. It is located in the Ames-Pleasant Valley-Royalview Drive area. This is an area using nature-derived names for streets, especially those based on trees.

ASPEN CIRCLE (C7)

Aspen Circle was dedicated on December 7, 1970, in Ordinance 352-70. This was part of the Pinehurst Subdivision. This street was named for a tree, as were most of the streets in this area.

AUGUSTINE DRIVE (F6)

Augustine Drive was dedicated on December 2, 1957, in Ordinance 327-57. This street was dedicated to Sylvester Augustine, who was Mayor of Parma from 1942 to 1945. He was also mayor from 1960 to 1961. He died in office. Mayor Augustine lived on Farnsworth Drive in Parma. (Information is from former Mayor James Day.)

AVALON DRIVE (G6)

Avalon Drive was dedicated by City Council on April 21, 1975 (City Ordinance 26-75). Avalon was the name of a town on Catalina Island, which is part of Los Angeles County. This town has a love song named after it which, according to the courts, was lifted from an Italian Opera by Puccini. Puccini sued in court and received $25,000. The court action made the song more popular. It is a love song about the town of Avalon on Catalina Island. The street's name could also come from an Arthurian legend which states that there is an earthly paradise island in the western seas named Avalon. Avalon Drive is located in the vicinity of Camelot Drive and Lancelot Drive, just north off Pleasant Valley Road off Meadow Lane. (Information on the song was taken from the *Family Song Book* by the Reader's Digest.)

Streets and Roads . . . .

Does the road wind up-hill all the way?
Yes, to the very end.
Will the day's journey take the whole long day?
From morn to night, my friend.

Christina Rossetti,
"Golden Hours"
pg. 1649-14

BAGLEY ROAD (A7)

There is a very short part of Bagley Road located in Parma, and that part was dedicated on April 19, 1954, in City Ordinance 63-54 (Engineer's Office). This small section of the road in Parma was changed to "East" Bagley Road. In Berea and Middleburg Heights, Bagley Road was dedicated in 1835. It was named after Abijah (alijah) (Aba) Bagley, who owned a home in the 1820's on what is now called Bagley Road. It was "the only place to rest the horses between Cleveland and Columbia." Bagley Road is thought to have been an original Indian trail. Previously this street was called Irish, Dutch, and Hamlin Roads. (Information is from the Berea Historical Society and Berea City Hall.)

BANNER LANE (D6)

Banner Lane was dedicated on July 22, 1957, in City Ordinance 195-57. Seltzer-Wickman-Stormes were the developers. This street was named after the Banner Construction Company, which belonged to George Seltzer (above) when he was in the home construction business in the early 1950's.

BARON DRIVE (B8)

This street was dedicated on November 6, 1968, in Parma City Ordinance 306-68. The Baron Development Company was involved in the 20th Century Homes Subdivision. Engineers were Charles McKinney and Associates. Mr. McKinney states that this street was named after a Parma Housing inspector in the 1960's, Erwin Behrend (Baron). Landowners were Ernest Nemeth and Julia Nemeth. Ron DeAnna was president of the company and Sidney Bailus was Secretary. This street is also located across York Road from the German Central Farm. Other streets in the area took on German names. Might not this street have been named for a German nobleman? Or could this street have been named after the company itself? Charles McKinney was the only person we found able to verify any information on this street. Could the name Behrend have been a factor in naming this street Baron Drive, after Mr. Behrend refused to have the street named after himself?

BARTON CIRCLE (D6)

This street was dedicated on January 17, 1966, in City Ordinance number 5-66. See below for further information.

BARTON HILLS DRIVE (D6)

This street was dedicated on July 3, 1961. The developers Stormes-Wickman-Seltzer named this street and the one above after Hazel Barton Seltzer, who was the wife of George Seltzer, one of the developers. Her maiden name was Barton. George died and eventually Hazel married again and moved to Scottsdale, Arizona. Information was furnished by Leonard Lane, a relative of the Stormes Family, who is the son of Trevor Lane, for which another street in this development was named.

BAUERDALE AVENUE (D2)

Bauerdale Avenue, which is located in the Evergreen Lake Area, off Pearl Road, was named after the family who owned the property, Frank and Catherine Bauer. Frank was also the developer. The street was dedicated on May 5, 1923, and recorded on June 13, 1923. It was part of the Lake Park Allotment. The Evergreen Lake area is a real nature area and a unique residential section of Parma.

BAVARIA ROAD (D3)

Bavaria Road was part of the Tuxedo Lake Overlook Allotments. This street was dedicated on April 21, 1924. It is one of a number of streets in the area named after German cities and areas in Germany. Owners of the land were Arthur Hoffman, Oswald Kobelt, Werner Kobelt, and Carrie Kobelt. (Information is from County Building Plat Book, Vol. 89, page 20.)

BEAU COURT (E6)

Beau Court was dedicated on January 6, 1969, in Ordinance 397-68 at the request of the developer, Julius Paris. He states that this name was picked for aesthetic reasons. He named a number of his streets with pleasant-sounding French names. With the last name of Paris this is understandable. Beau is a French word meaning beautiful, fashionable, or a handsome suitor or lover.

BELMERE DRIVE (D4)

Belmere Drive was dedicated on June 28, 1922. This street is part of the H. A. Stahl Development. It appears H. A. Stahl applied many of the ideas in Parma that were used in setting up Shaker Heights using the Garden City philosophy. Included are winding roads, lakes, and a golf course. The street names were taken from Shaker Heights streets or taken from the same English source from which the Shaker Heights streets were named, the Garden Cities of England in the 1920's. H. A. Stahl lived in Shaker Heights in the 1920's and had an office at Cedar and Coventry Roads. Belmere means Beautiful (Bel) apart from anything else (mere). (See in this book "H. A. Stahl, A Tribute." Information is from County Archives.)

BERESFORD AVENUE (A7)

This street was dedicated on October 7, 1957, in Ordinance 249-57; however, it was dedicated in Parma Heights on May 6, 1929. It was part of the Briar Cliff Subdivision. S. H. Kleinman Realty was the developer. There is a town in southern England, just north of Wareham, England, called Bere Regis. There is a man by the name of Sir Richard de la Bere who has his coat of arms mentioned in the book *The Romance of Heraldry* by Wilfrid Scott-Giles. Could Beresford be a derivative of Bere or could it be named after Beresford Square, the town center in Woolwich, a section of London? This information is from the Internet. However, no further information could be found to substantiate this. Some investigation is still being carried out on this matter.

BERTHA AVENUE (D3)

Bertha Avenue was dedicated on March 9, 1923, and recorded on April 30, 1923. Frank Lander was the engineer for the Tuxedo Orchard Allotment development. The property owners were Freida and John Kobelt. After a few years of research, it was discovered that the land was purchased by the developer from the Schmotzer family on July 6, 1917, and the Resnik family on August 1, 1917. Both families had women named Bertha. This could not be verified, but it is a very strong assumption that this street was named after these women: Bertha Schmotzer and Bertha Resnik. This information was secured from the County Plat map Parma Book, 1916 to 1925, at the County Archives Center on Franklin Avenue on May 19, 1994.

BICENTENNIAL DRIVE (B7)

In 1976, the United States celebrated its 200th birthday. Bicentennial Drive (a park street) was dedicated by Mayor John Petruska to celebrate this occasion.

BIG CREEK PARKWAY (C2)

Big Creek Parkway was dedicated at Brookpark Road on June 18, 1953, in City Ordinance 88-53. This dedication was with the Knollwood and Westview Drives apartment developments. The Metroparks were started in 1917, the year in which this street was dedicated as a park. Big Creek Parkway is bordered by the above apartment complexes on the east side of the road and the wooded Big Creek Reservation on the west. As the Parkway heads south, it winds through the woods of the Big Creek Reservation. The homes and roads running off to the east (namely, Fernhill Avenue, Pinegrove Avenue, West Moreland Road and Oakdale Road) have a very natural, scenic setting. (See picture 53.)

BISCAYNE BOULEVARD (G7)

Biscayne Boulevard is part of the Richard Plat Subdivision. It was dedicated on December 5, 1966, in Ordinance 425-66. This street is part of the first group of streets named after Florida locations. The Broad-Valle Subdivision in the same area had many streets named after Florida locations. Biscayne Boulevard is a well-known street in Miami, Florida.

BOBKO BOULEVARD (B7)

This street was named after John A. Bobko, who was a councilman from 1956 to 1961. He was mayor immediately after the death of Mayor Sylvester Augustine in 1961. Mr. Bobko also ran a restaurant on State Road which was a gathering place for local politicians and other public figures. His restaurant was located at the corner of Grovewood Avenue and State Road. The same building is there now. The windows were bricked in for the bar it is now. Bobko Boulevard was dedicated on September 2, 1958, in Ordinance 250-58. (Information is from former Mayor James Day, March 24, 1989.)

BONNY BOULEVARD (F7)

Chuck Wagner, a Forest City official, stated that the street was named after Bonny Builders, a developer in the area. The street was dedicated on December 3, 1956, in Ordinance 291-56 (City Hall File).

BOUNDARY LANE (C7)

Boundary Lane was dedicated on January 19, 1959, in Ordinance 10-59. It is the boundary between Parma and Parma Heights, located off York Road.

BOWMAN LANE (F7)

Bowman Lane, which is located in the "Robinhood Development," was dedicated on March 9, 1964, in City Ordinance 52-64. This seems to be named in accordance with the theme of the streets in the area: "The Robinhood Tales." This was a Richard MacKay Development.

BRADENTON BOULEVARD (F7)

Bradenton Boulevard was dedicated on January 15, 1962, in Ordinance 3-62 by City Council at the request of Bonny Builders. It is another street named in the two "Florida Estates." After James Day, former councilman-at-large and mayor, arrived back from a Florida vacation, he suggested the names of Florida cities be given to the streets in Parma's Southern Hills area. (See Winterpark Drive for further information.)

BRADLEY AVENUE (D2)

Bradley Avenue was named after the Alfred and Clarissa Bradley Family. They owned the land where the street is now located before the turn of the century. Their daughter, Mary Ann Bradley, was the paternal grandmother to Dr. Dudley Fay, who gave the historical society this information. The street was dedicated on July 16, 1917. It is located five blocks south of Brookpark Road between Pearl Road and West 54th Street. (See picture 48.)

BRAINARD DRIVE (B2)

Brainard Drive, located in the Hauserman Road and Snow Road area, is not named after the more notable Brainard family as one might suspect. According to Ben Brainard, an early Cleveland Trust banker in the area, the land where this street is located was owned by two women named Brainard and a man named Henry Brainard. They were not related to Ben Brainard, our informant. They bought this land and lived on it for 30 years but could not farm it successfully. This was in the 1920's and 1930's. Ben said he had dealings with them at the bank. It is believed that when they sold the property, they moved to Vermont. The street was dedicated on August 24, 1927, and recorded on September 22, 1927. In 1989, at the time of this interview, Ben Brainard was 91, and he and his wife were still living in Brookpark, Ohio.

BREMEN AVENUE (D2)

Bremen Avenue is located in Tuxedo Lake Overlook Allotments. Within this allotment, a number of streets were named after German cities. One of the owners of the land was Arthur Hoffman. The street was dedicated on April 21, 1924, and recorded on November 15, 1924. This is sometimes referred to as the "German allotment." Other owners were Oswald Kobelt, Werner Kobelt and Carrie Kobelt. None of the relatives of the Kobelt family knew why the streets were named after German cities. (County Vol. 89, page 20.) (See picture 34.)

BRIAN DRIVE (F8)

Nelson Builders were involved in the naming of this street. It was named after a five-year-old boy named Brian Nelson by his grandfather, Hugh Nelson, Sr. Brian is presently living in Long Beach, California, and working for General Motors. Brian was born in 1962. His grandfather, Hugh Nelson, Sr., was president of Nelson Homes Inc. until his death in 1969. Brian's father, Hugh Nelson, Jr., became president until his death in 1977 at age 40. Nelson Homes Inc. then disappeared. Brian Drive was dedicated on July 8, 1970, in Ordinance 207-70. (Information received from Sharon Nelson, mother of Brian, June 13, 1989.)

BRITTANY DRIVE (7E)

Brittany Drive was dedicated on March 18, 1996, by City Council at the request of Councilman Paul T. Kirner. It seems Mr. Kirner was picked as godfather to Councilman Kelley's new baby girl, Brittany, and Kirner asked council to have the only remaining numbered street in his Ward, West 58th Street, to be named Brittany Drive.

BROADROCK COURT (G2)

Though it might not be immediately apparent, this street seemed to be named after its location. It is a street one block north of Old Rockside (which was Rockside Road in 1956) and runs off Broadview, hence the name Broadrock Court. It is a relatively new street for this area,

having been dedicated on June 24, 1955, and recorded on January 20, 1956. Another dedication date is given as June 24, 1957, in Ordinance 107-57. It is located near the 1849 Henninger Home, a truly historic piece of property. The developer was Jules Keller, and the development was called Broadrock Subdivision. (County Vol. 166, page 27.)

BROAD-VALLE DRIVE (G7)

This street was dedicated on April 17, 1961, in Ordinance 57-61. It seems that its location near Broadview Road and Pleasant Valley Road is the reason for its name. This was part of the Broad Valle subdivision. Another street in the area appears to have been named after its location, and that was Hillcrest Lane. The hill behind Pleasant Valley and Broadview is a prominent feature of the land.

BROADVIEW ROAD (G2)

Broadview Road has had a number of names. It was first called Town Line Road, separating Parma Township from Independence Township, and it was also known as Independence Road. In Cleveland, Broadview Road was called Broad Street because it was the broadest street around. Word has it that as you climbed the hill in Parma you had quite a view of Broad Street from the top of the hill, and it became Broadview Road. Points of interest: Broadview Hill at one time was known as Herbst Hill, according to Emily (Wessell) Ahlers. The Johnson House was built on the corner of Broadview Road and Pearl Road in 1892. It was built by John L. Johnson, grandfather to the future Mayor of Parma, Frank D. Johnson. Before that, the Country Hotel was located at the same site. Broadview Road was a toll road at one time. (Information from *History of Parma* by Ernest Kubasek.) The Henninger Home, built in 1849, is still standing on the corner of Old Rockside Road and Broadview. Broadview Road became a county road in 1820 and became a state road in 1828. Broadview Road became State Route 176 on August 20, 1947. (See pictures 41 and 47.)

BROOKDALE AVENUE (A3)

Brookdale Avenue was partially dedicated on January 3, 1923, at the request of E. Moran, the developer. Its close association to Brooklyn and Brooklyn Heights is probably the reason for its name. West of Broadview Road, this street was originally called Overlook Avenue. That section was changed to Brookdale on November 9, 1925, in Ordinance 135. (See picture 45.)

BROOKPARK ROAD (Gl)

The history of Brookpark Road is very interesting. In 1831 Robert Davis, Benajah Fay, Isaac Robinson and Warren Young petitioned the County Commissioners to set up Brookpark Road. Here are the reasons they gave: (1) To open the way for settlers through a wolf-infested wilderness; (2) To open communications between two important sections of the County (Brooklyn and Berea). The Commissioners heard the request, and Brookpark Road was opened from the northwest corner of Parma (Rockport) to Berea Road in 1843. The next section was opened from Berea Road to Grayton Road in 1896. Then in 1912 an extension was made from Wooster Parkway (Pearl Road) to Schaaf Road. In 1922 Brookpark Road was extended south of Schaaf Road to the Cuyahoga Valley. It became State Route 17 on August 20, 1947. According to W. F. Holzworth, who wrote the *History of Brook Park Village*, Brookpark Road was originally called Townline Road in the Brookpark area, where it was the boundary between Middleburg Township and Rockport Township. (Thanks to Elma Gifford and the North Olmsted Area Historical Society, we have been able to give the above account of the establishment of Brookpark Road. Sharon Guinaugh of the Fairview Park Historical Society is the person who led us to the North Olmsted Area Historical Society. Thanks to both societies for their help and to Sharon and Elma. This information was secured from a dedication booklet of the Brookpark Bridge or Viaduct [1934]. Parma's Mayor A. A. Fleger [see Fleger Drive] was at the dedication.)

BROOKVIEW BOULEVARD (Fl)

Brookview Boulevard runs off Broadview Road into Brooklyn Heights, where it is the first street from Brookpark Road and is in *view* of Brooklyn Heights, Ohio. The owners of the property were Christian and Clara Huy. It was part of the Klein/Lampl Company's Brookview Subdivision. This street is one street from Brookpark Road and runs off Broadview Road, which could be the reason for its name. The street was dedicated on December 21, 1924. It was recorded on July 15, 1924. Other parts of the street were dedicated on June 8, 1925, by the Homesite Company (County Vol. 78, page 25). (See pictures 42 - 47.)

BROWNFIELD DRIVE (D3)

Brownfield Drive was dedicated on June 24, 1921, in the H. A. Stahl Ridgewood Plat #1. The exact date of dedication is not known in Parma Township records, but the County Engineer accepted the plat on the above date. According to Mrs. Virginia Brown Fox (DOB 7-28-1912) of Tampa, Florida, this street might have been named after her father, Thomas B. Brown, the Sales Director of the H. A. Stahl Company. She does not know this for sure if this is how the name was arrived at, but it is the most likely assumption. Virginia Avenue, in fact, was named after her. Streets were named by H. A. Stahl, and most of these names were from the Garden Cities of England in the 1920's; however, a few streets were named by Mr. Stahl's associates, and they named them after relatives. (See, for example, Kenneth Avenue.) The Brown name was well known in the area for many years. Marcus A. Brown owned land in Parma in 1892, and E. M. Brown owned land in 1903. They both owned land on the southeast corner of what is now the intersection of Ridge Road and Ridgewood Drive, but there is no indication that this street was named after them. Could it have been? Good question! You take your pick. (See in this book "H. A. Stahl, A Tribute" for further information.)

BRUENING DRIVE (E5)

Bruening Drive was originally dedicated on May 21, 1956, in Ordinance 95-56 as Chestnut Avenue, but a short time later, on October 22, 1956, in Ordinance 253-56, it was changed to Bruening Drive by City Council. According to former Mayor James Day and residents Anna Bandow and Rita Budd, the street was named after the Bruening family, who owned property in the area. Dr. Bruening was a very popular physician. He had his office in the Broadview Road/Pearl Road area. The Bruening family owned the home on the corner of State Road and Bruening Drive. There was another street called Chestnut Drive (Evergreen Lake area) which might have been the cause for changing the name of this street. (Information is from City Hall.)

BUCKINGHAM DRIVE (D4)

This street is part of the H. A. Stahl Development. It appears that H. A. Stahl applied many of the ideas in Parma that were used in setting up Shaker Heights, collectively referred to as the Garden City philosophy. Included in this concept are the winding roads, lakes, and golf courses. The street names were taken from Shaker Heights streets or taken from the same English source from which the Shaker Heights streets were named, the Garden Cities of England in the 1920's. H. A. Stahl lived in Shaker Heights in the 1920's and had an office at Cedar and Coventry Roads. (See in this book "H. A. Stahl, A Tribute" for further information.) Buckingham Drive was dedicated as a street on November 2, 1923. It crosses Ridge Road just south of Parma Circle (Ridgewood Circle). Besides Buckingham Palace, there is a small town north of London, England, in Buckinghamshire called Buckingham. It seems to be the main city in Buckinghamshire (*shire* on the end of a name indicates a governmental district or a district with some official status). It might be noted that there is a street named Buckingham Avenue in Lakeland, Florida, where the Cleveland Heights Country Club is located–another of H. A. Stahl's developments. (See picture 2 on page 24.)

BURDEN DRIVE (F7)

This street was named after Tom Burden, the Engineer for Bonny Builders. The street was dedicated on December 3, 1956, by City Council at the request of Bonny Builders. (Ordinance 291-56). Information is from William DeGraeve of Bonny Builders, September 11, 1996.

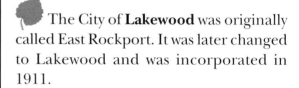

Did you know that . . . .

The City of **Lakewood** was originally called East Rockport. It was later changed to Lakewood and was incorporated in 1911.

The City of **Massillon**, founded in 1826, was founded by James Duncan and Ferdinand Hurxthal. It was named after Jean Baptiste Massillon (1663-1742), a French clergyman whose sermons were Mrs. Duncan's favorite reading. Massillon was incorporated as a town in 1838.

The City of **Barberton** was founded in 1891 by O. C. Barber and was named after its founder.

The City of **Kent**, settled in 1805, was named after Zenas Kent, who purchased property in the area in 1832. This town was originally known as Franklin Mills. Aaron Olmsted of Hartford, Connecticut, named it Franklin after his son. A relative of Mr. Kent, Marvin Kent, became Governor of Ohio. Kent was incorporated in 1920.

OHIO PLACE NAMES by Larry L. Miller
University of Indiana Press, 1996

CAMBRIDGE DRIVE (Cl)

This street was named after Cambridge University in England; the latter was founded in the 13th century. The reason for this credible assumption is that in this particular development all streets were named after institutions of learning, and at least three were found in England. Cambridge Drive was dedicated on November 6, 1961, in City Ordinance 200-61. (See the entry for Harrow Drive for further discussion.) There is also the city of Cambridge, Massachusetts, a suburb of Boston, where Harvard University is located. But there is no reason to believe this city had anything to do with the naming of this street.

CAMELOT DRIVE (G7)

Camelot Drive is located in an area where there is a group of streets named after legendary English heroes and places. The street was dedicated on October 3, 1966, in City Ordinance 121-66. Camelot is the legendary paradise where King Arthur and his knights of the round table had their headquarters. It has been said by some to have been located in the area of Monmouth (see Monmouth Drive in this book), a city on the border of Wales and England. Some say it was located in the Glastonbury area where a few other city names have the name Camel. No one has ever been able to locate positively the site of the famed city of Camelot. (Information is from *Place Names of the English Speaking World* by C. M. Matthews.

CANTERBURY DRIVE (D4)

Canterbury Drive was dedicated on June 28, 1922 (North Canterbury Road), by Parma Township at the request of H. A. Stahl, Parma's first major developer. It appears that H. A. Stahl applied many of the ideas in Parma that were used in setting up the Garden Cities of the early 1900's. He incorporated winding roads, lakes, and a golf course. The street names were taken from Shaker Heights, a typical Garden city, or taken from the same English source from which the Shaker Heights' streets were named, the

Garden Cities of England of the early 1900's. H. A. Stahl lived in Shaker Heights in the 1920's where many of the developers in Parma lived at this time. He had an office at Cedar and Coventry Roads. (See in this book "H. A. Stahl, A Tribute" for further information.) Canterbury is the name of a city located on the southeastern tip of England. It is noted for its cathedral and has been the headquarters of the Church in England for centuries. South Canterbury Road was dedicated on March 26, 1924. Both streets are located off Parma Circle, north and south. (See pictures 14, 15, 16, 19 and 35.)

CARLTON ROAD (G3)

Carlton Road was named after Carl Henninger (1881 - 1940). He owned the property where this street is now located. The street was dedicated on April 6, 1959, in City Ordinance 52-59. (Information is from Jan Henninger.)

CECILIA DRIVE (G8)

Cecilia Drive is located in the Green Valley/Parma Woods Estates, located south of Normandy High School. This street is named after a unique individual. City Council named this street after Cecilia Lehr for her many years of work for the Democratic party in the city of Parma. Cecilia Drive was dedicated on October 2, 1967, in Ordinance 213-67. John Lehr and his wife, Cecilia, moved to Parma in 1927 to their Lincoln Avenue home. In 1928, she became a charter member of the Parma Democratic Club. Her 54 years of work for the Democratic Party include many interesting achievements. She was elected president of the Parma Women's Democratic Club in the 1930's. Hanratty's Barn was the location of her many fund raising activities. The barn was located near the playground at the corner of West 54th Street and Snow Road. Her husband, John, who died in 1973, was also active in Parma politics. As an aside, the street was originally dedicated as *Cecelia,* but on July 7, 1969, in Ordinance 247-69 it was changed by council to *Cecilia,* (City Hall).

CELESTE DRIVE (B8)

Celeste Drive was named after Celeste Wenz, councilman Allan Wenz's 13-year-old daughter. She is now Celeste Survoy. He was councilman of Ward 7 in 1966-1967. This street was originally dedicated on February 20, 1961, as West 114th Street. The name was changed to Celeste Drive on February 6, 1967, in Ordinance 441-66. (Information is from Lorie Eckman, a school friend of Celeste.)

CENTER DRIVE (F5)

This street was part of the Chestnut Heights Allotment, which included Park Drive, Overlook Drive (now Stanfield Drive), Esper Avenue, Jourden Avenue and Lyle Avenue. Lillian Helper, the named owner of the land and the wife of the developer, could not give a reason for this street having been named Center Drive. The most plausible explanation is that this street is the center street of the three developed (Park Drive, Center Drive and Overlook Drive). Center Drive was dedicated on October 15, 1924.

CHARLES AVENUE (D3)

This street presents a particular problem: which came first, the chicken or the egg? St. Charles Parish, which is on the corner of Charles Avenue and Ridge Road, was started in 1923, and Charles Avenue was dedicated on October 24, 1922. But streets are generally named after the establishment of the church. The Catholic Diocese owned the land under the name of Archbishop Joseph Schrembs (1866-1945) in 1922. It appears that the land for Wilber Avenue (the next street north) was sold to H. A. Stahl in 1923 or 1922 since Wilber Avenue was dedicated on October 12, 1923. Mr. Stahl might have been aware of the church being considered for this location. Then again, neither the parish nor the street might be the cause for the name Charles. There was a civil engineer named Charles Root, who worked on the layout of the street. Naming a street after an engineer or other officials would not be unusual. Neither the Diocese, the parish, nor the City of Parma has the answer.

CHATEAU DRIVE (C7)

This street was originally dedicated on May 20, 1957, in Ordinance 107-57 as West 96th Street. On June 26, 1962, in Ordinance 79-62, the residents had the name changed to Chateau Drive. No resident could be found who knew why the name Chateau was picked. The word is French and it means a large country estate or a French vineyard estate. The name seems to fit this street well with its suburban look. (See picture 50.)

CHESTERFIELD AVENUE (D2)

Chesterfield Avenue was dedicated on January 20, 1923. It was part of the Tuxedo Heights Allotment. Chesterfield Avenue is a very long street, and some of the homes, front porch colonials, were built in the 1920's. Brookpark Realty was the developer. D. A. Loftus and William Pitts were the officers. The developers in Parma during the 1920's named their streets after English place names. There is a town in England called Chesterfield in Derbyshire County. Though cigarettes were starting to be produced in 1910 as we know them today, it is doubtful that the streets in this area were named after cigarettes as some would like to think.

CHESTNUT DRIVE (D2)

Chestnut Drive seems to have received its name sometime after the dedication of Evergreen Lake streets. It is a small street and it runs from Westmoreland Drive to Evergreen Drive. It is part of the Tuxedo Lake Park allotment. This street was dedicated in late August 1919, probably on the 28th. It was developed by Frank Johnson. Another street in Parma had this name but was changed to Bruening Drive. Bruening Drive had this name only from May 21, 1956, to October 22, 1956. The change was made because of the above-named street.

CHESTNUT HILLS DRIVE (D3 and D4)

This street was dedicated in two sections. The west side was dedicated on December 12, 1923, and the east half was dedicated on June 28, 1922. Another dedication date was given on March 26, 1924. It is believed the first two were the official dedication dates. This street is part of the H. A. Stahl Development. It appears that H. A. Stahl applied all the ideas to Parma that were used in setting up Shaker Heights: namely, the Garden City philosophy that included the winding roads, lakes, and a golf course. The street names were taken from Shaker Heights streets or taken from the same English source from which the Shaker Heights streets were named, the Garden Cities of England in the 1920's. H. A. Stahl lived in Shaker Heights in the 1920's and had an office at Cedar and Coventry Roads. (See in this book "H. A. Stahl, A Tribute" for further information.) Chestnut Hills Drive runs through Parma Circle (Ridgewood Circle) from northwest at Snow Road to the southeast at Hollywood Drive at the Ridgewood Golf Course. It is a very attractive area of Parma.

CHEVROLET BOULEVARD (B2)

Chevrolet Boulevard was called Stumph(f) Road originally. However, where the Chevrolet Plant is located it was changed to Chevrolet Boulevard. This was done on July 6, 1972, in City Ordinance 203-72. This street was actually the Stumph family's driveway to their farm from Brookpark Road in the early days. (See Stumph(f) Road for further information.)

CLEARVIEW AVENUE (G3)

Clearview Avenue seems to have been named for aesthetic purposes. It was dedicated on March 21, 1927, and recorded on May 17, 1927. Could this street also be named after its location, as other streets in the area were? Meadowlawn Boulevard and Parkleigh Drive–both refer to clearings or open fields. This street was part of the Dartmoor Subdivision #2, developed by the K.L. Land Company: R. C. Johnson, Vice President, and Jack Lampl,

Secretary (County Vol. 105, page 38). For more Information, see Parkleigh Drive.

CLEARWATER DRIVE (F8)

Located in the southern hills of Parma, Clearwater Drive was one of a number of streets in the area named after Florida cities during the 1960's and 1970's. This was just about the time people became retirement conscious, and Florida was a great place to retire. Former Mayor James Day, when he was Councilman-at-large, started the trend when he returned from a vacation in Florida. He suggested Florida names for new streets. Clearwater Drive was dedicated October 2, 1978, by City Ordinance 210-78.

COCOA DRIVE (F8)

Cocoa Drive is part of one of the two Florida Estates located in the southern hills of Parma. It seems Florida place names were very popular at the time when many people started talking about retirement. When Former Mayor James Day was Councilman-at-large in 1960, he started the trend. When returning from a Florida vacation, he suggested the Florida names for new streets. Cocoa Drive was dedicated on May 19, 1980, in City Ordinance 162-79.

COMMERCE PARKWAY WEST (B1)

Commerce Parkway West was dedicated on June 21, 1982, in Ordinance 621-82. It is located in the northwest part of Parma off Brookpark Road at about 10500 Brookpark Road. It is like a modern commerce parkway with new buildings and neat surroundings.

COMMONWEALTH DRIVE (F3)

Commonwealth Drive was dedicated on March 3, 1923, by Parma Township for Elworthy/Helwick Developers. This is a street developed by Donald Helwick. He was a resident of Cleveland Heights and must have known others who lived in the Cleveland Heights-Shaker Heights Area who were developing what were known as the Garden Cities. Garden Cities were first developed in England and were special communities set aside from the big cities for what we would call suburban living. These men not only set up communities to this order but also used the names they found in or around these original Garden Communities. The above street is a good example. This was called the Guilford Park Allotment. Don S. Helwick was president. Other streets dedicated were Heresford Drive, Sedgwick Avenue (now a numbered street) and Malverne Avenue (also a numbered street), West 32nd and West 29th. Both Sedgwick Avenue and Malverne Avenue are street names in Shaker Heights. There is a town just south of London called Guildford.

CONCORD DRIVE (Private) (E4)

This is a private street containing some unique rows of townhouses. There are about 260 units. It is about one-half mile long and borders State Road Park and Ridgewood Golf Course. For condominium living it is one of the best. These townhouses were built in the 1960's and 1970's.

CORAL GABLES DRIVE (F8)

Coral Gables Drive was dedicated on October 2, 1978, in Ordinance 210-78. It is part of the "two Florida Estates" located in the southern hills of Parma. This was one of the last streets named after Florida cities. It was during the 1960's and 1970's during the first Florida trend that most of these streets were first named. Retirement in Florida was becoming popular. Former Mayor James Day, when he was Councilman-at-large in 1960, started this trend when he returned from a Florida vacation and suggested Florida names for new streets.

COTTONWOOD LANE (C7)

Cottonwood Lane was dedicated on December 7, 1970. It was part of the Pinehurst Subdivision #1. The cottonwood tree is a very fast growing tree, and it does provide shade quickly for a new home. It grows very tall and with the exception that it sheds a white cotton-like material in the spring of the year, it is a handsome tree. It must be a nice tree as Livingston and Evans used the tree in their song "Tammy," which Debbie Reynolds sang in the movie *Tammy and the Bachelor*. The words go: "I hear the Cottonwoods whisp'rin' above, Tammy, Tammy." What more can be said for a tree that has taken a bum rap for so many years? Tammy is not the only one who liked cottonwood trees. There was a man who lived on Brian Drive here in Parma who raised a cottonwood tree from 2 inches to 30 feet in 8 years, and it provided shade for his deck. However, the neighbors weren't all that thrilled about the tree. When this man moved, the neighbors got together with the new owners and they decided to chop the tree down. However, when they chopped the tree down, it fell the wrong way and hit the house and deck causing some minor damage; interesting!

COVENTRY DRIVE (F7)

Coventry Drive was most likely named after the city of Coventry, England, which is located about 15 miles from Birmingham, England. Coventry Drive is also located in what might be called the Robinhood and King Arthur Estates area off Pleasant Valley Road. Coventry Drive was dedicated on December 1, 1964, in Ordinance 272-64.

COVINGTON DRIVE (D4)

Covington Drive was originally dedicated as Ingleside Drive on March 26, 1924, at the request of H. A. Stahl. On January 18, 1932, the name was changed to Covington Drive. It seems there were two streets by the name of Ingleside. The other is located two blocks south of Snow Road off State Road. The name Covington is the name of a small town in England which is about 30 miles east-southeast of the town of Coventry. Sounds alike? Well, we have streets in Parma named after both, and this sound similarity could create confusion also.

CRAIGLEIGH DRIVE (D8)

Craigleigh Drive was dedicated on January 1, 1959, in Ordinance 2-59 by City Council. It was developed by the Craig Building Company, which was founded by John Craig (1898-1976) and his son Donald R. Craig (1922-1989). The company began in 1946 and closed its doors in 1964 when John retired. Donald, his son, went into the banking business at that time. Their office was located on Pearl Road. This particular development was called Ridgeview Estates. Craigleigh is located off Ridge Road one block south of Sprague. Family members couldn't give any reason for the *leigh* on the end of the name; however, in a book of *English Place Names* by C.M. Matthews, we learn that *leigh* in English was generally used in reference to a clearing or open space, and it was used as a suffix. An example would be the town of Cranleigh. Some of the above information was secured from Donald J. Craig, grandson to John Craig. For additional information on the word *leigh*, see Parkleigh Avenue.

CROSSLINE DRIVE (E7)

This street was dedicated on September 3, 1963, in Ordinance 183-63. It would seem it received its name from its location. It runs, so to speak, crossways between Sandy Hook Drive and Woodbury Hills Drive. It is in a very attractive neighborhood and is a part of Woodbury Hills Subdivision.

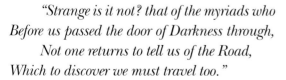

Streets and Roads . . . .

"Strange is it not? that of the myriads who Before us passed the door of Darkness through, Not one returns to tell us of the Road, Which to discover we must travel too."

Rubaiyat of Omar Khayyam, trans. Edward FitzGerald

DALESIDE DRIVE (F1)

This street has posed quite a problem. We have had conflicting reports that Daleside and Roseside Drives were named after children of the Henningers, the owners of the property. In our research we could not find children in the Henninger family named Rose and Dale. We have really not been able to verify anything from the living relatives of the families of Uhinck (other owners of this property) and the Henningers except that the Henningers say they never heard of the names in their family. Some members of the Uhinck family thought they were children of the Henninger family. No members of the developers' families, Van DeBoe and W. W. Hager, could be located. The owners were Roman Henninger, Ed Henninger, Nellie Henninger and Anna Uhinck. Daleside Drive was dedicated on April 20, 1918. The three streets in this development (Roseside Drive, Daleside Drive and Woodway Avenue) were laid out in a unique way. At the intersection of Daleside, Roseside and Woodway there is a large open area, intersecting streets and lawns, which gives the neighborhood a very attractive and spacious appearance. Information came from Uhinck family relatives and Henninger family relatives. (See picture 42.)

DARTMOOR AVENUE (G3)

Records show that this street was dedicated on November 10, 1926 (County Plat Book Vol. 101 and 102), at the request of the K & L Land Company (Klein & Lampl). It was during this period that many streets were named after English place names. There is a park in England called Dartmoor National Park located on the southwest tip of England about 10 miles north of the city of Plymouth. This street name is also found in the Cleveland Heights/Shaker Heights area where many of the street names in Parma were taken from in the 1920's. In English the word "moor" means an uncultivated parcel of land or marsh land. Dart is the name of a river in England. (Information is from *Meaning of English Place Names* by Harrington, page 18, and *Place Names of the English Speaking World*, by C. M.

Matthews.) R. C. Johnson and Jack Lampl were officers in the K & L Land Company.

DARTMOUTH DRIVE (D2)

Dartmouth Drive was dedicated on November 6, 1961, in Ordinance 200-61. This street is located with a group of streets which are named after institutions of learning which were elite types of schools, like Dartmouth College of the Ivy League. (See Roedean Drive for further information.) The ranch homes on Dartmouth have large front lawns and tree lawns which are impressive. There is a small town in England called Dartmouth, which is located south of Dartmoor National Park. It is at the mouth of the Dart River. (See also Dartworth Drive.)

DARTWORTH DRIVE (D3)

Dartworth was dedicated on October 22, 1924. This street is part of the H. A. Stahl Development. It appears H. A. Stahl applied to Parma all the Garden City ideas that were used in setting up Shaker Heights: they included the winding roads, lakes, and a golf course. The street names were taken from Shaker Heights streets or taken from the same English sources from which the Shaker Heights streets were named, that is, the Garden Cities of England in the 1910's. H. A. Stahl lived in Shaker Heights in the 1920's and had an office at Cedar and Coventry Roads. (See in this book "H. A. Stahl, A Tribute" for further information.) This street, like some of the other street names picked by H. A. Stahl, has a classic English name. Part of Dartworth Drive, east of Ridge Road, was originally called Greenlawn Drive, and was dedicated on January 17, 1923. It was changed to Dartworth Drive on December 29, 1933, in Ordinance 158. This name *Dartworth* comes from two words: "Dart," a river, and "Worth," a farm enclosure. It seems, then, that this street name means a river running through a farm enclosure. Then again, "Worth" could be a

family surname. (Information is from *Place Names of the English Speaking World,* pages 337 and 18, by C. M. Matthews.) (See picture 30.)

DAVID DRIVE (G8)

One could say that David Drive has actually two people who are honored by the naming of this street. The first was David Marusa, who was the son of Albert Marusa, developer and owner of this property on the Broadview Road end of David Drive. The date of this dedication was December 17, 1962 (information from Parma City Hall). The second person was David Nelson, the grandson of Hugh John Nelson, Sr., president of Nelson Homes Inc. (see Brian Drive for further information on the Nelson Family). The second half, the western half of David Drive, was dedicated on December 1, 1964, in Ordinance 173-64. Both streets had different origins even though they are connected.

DAWN HAVEN DRIVE (B7)

Dawn Haven Drive was dedicated on May 5, 1958, in Ordinance 124-58 as West 119th Street. This street was actually named by the residents after they lived on the street for four years. It was named in 1962. Betty Kruse, a resident, said she came up with the name because the street looked so quiet and pretty in the morning sunlight. The residents voted on this name, one of three from which they had to pick. This street is located in the Ann Arbor Drive area. It was dedicated Dawn Haven Drive on September 4, 1962.

DAWN VISTA OVAL (E6)

Dawn Vista Oval was dedicated on December 17, 1979, in Ordinance 190-79. It was named by the Sunrise Builders, which might account for the name of the street. In this development some of the most attractive names were used, such as Night Vista Drive and Eventide Drive. This street name, as well as the others, could be described as an aesthetic name.

DAWNSHIRE DRIVE (E3)

Dawnshire Drive runs off State Road and stops about two blocks from West 54th Street. If it continued straight through to West 54th Street, it would be the continuation of Morningside Drive. This is an interesting observation but probably has no connection to the naming of this street. Records do not indicate why this street was called Dawnshire. *Shire* is an English name which means a governmental area like our county. However, a Dawnshire could not be found in England as such. William and Maud Loesch were the owners of this land when the Parmawood Company purchased it. The street was dedicated on March 8, 1926. (Information is from County Plat book.)

DAWNWOOD DRIVE (G3)

The owners and developers of this property were John and Maggie Buhl. This was called the Dawnwood Subdivision. Dawnwood Drive was dedicated on November 10, 1926. (Information is from County Plat Map Book 445 Vol. 101, page 29.) As far as can be determined, this is just an aesthetic name.

DAY DRIVE (D5)

Former Parma Mayor James W. Day, 1962 to 1967, received the honor of having this street named after him. He was active in politics many years prior to his election as mayor. Day Drive was dedicated on July 21, 1958, in Ordinance 225-58. He was mayor during the second expansion era and was very helpful in providing much information for this study. (Information is from Parma City Hall.)

DAYTONA DRIVE (G8)

Daytona Drive was dedicated on April 17, 1961, in Ordinance 57-61. It is part of the "Florida Estates." It seems that Councilman-at-large James Day, soon to be mayor, had just returned from a vacation in Florida and suggested these streets be named after Florida cities. Daytona Beach is located about 50 miles north of Cape Canaveral.

DEBBY DRIVE (A7)

Debby Drive was dedicated on September 2, 1958. This was a Marvin Gross Subdivision. The street was named after Marvin Gross's teenage daughter, Debby Gross. (Information is from City Hall records and from Marvin Gross.)

DEBORAH DRIVE (B2)

Deborah Drive was dedicated on June 23, 1954, in Resolution Number 113-54 by Parma City Council. The street was named after Deborah Ratner, young daughter of Albert Ratner of the Forest City Enterprises. Deborah Drive has an interesting triangular traffic island at the intersection of Elizabeth Drive, which gives an attractive setting for the area.

DECKER DRIVE (H3)

Decker Drive was dedicated, in Parma, on December 7, 1959, in Ordinance 215-59 by Al Rispo, the developer. The Seven Hills part of the street was named earlier by Julius Paris. This street was named after the Decker family, who owned the property. This same Decker family owned a hardware business at the turn of the century in old Brooklyn at West 25th (Pearl Road) and Broadview. This street was named after them. August and Christine Decker were the owners of the hardware business. John Decker, their son, owned the land where Decker Drive now stands. Marian Wurm, our informant, is a niece to John Decker. Her father, Arthur Decker, was John Decker's brother. (Information received from Marian Wurm on April 4, 1996.)

DEER RUN TRAIL (C7)

This street was dedicated on July 7, 1980, in Ordinance 114-79. The way deer were running around Parma at that time, it is no wonder someone would come up with the name Deer Run Trail. The streets in this area have very attractive names. This is a short street that is just south of Pleasant Valley Lake in the Fox Hollow Drive area.

DEERFIELD DRIVE (D3)

Deerfield Drive was dedicated on March 26, 1924, by Parma Township. This street is part of the H. A. Stahl Development. It appears that H. A. Stahl applied the Garden City philosophy in Parma that the Van Sweringen Brothers did in Shaker Heights. They used the winding roads, lakes, and a golf course. The street names were taken from Shaker Heights streets or taken from the same English source from which the Shaker Heights streets were named, the Garden Cities of England in the 1920's. H. A. Stahl lived in Shaker Heights in the 1920's and had an office at Cedar and Coventry Roads. (See in this book "H. A. Stahl, A Tribute" for further information.) Parma still has deer running wild within the city limits. This is a very appropriate name since deer must have been running all through this area at that time. Eleven suburbs have used this name in naming their streets. The Deerfield name was also used by H. A. Stahl in the naming of a street in his Cleveland Heights Community in Lakeland, Florida.

DELL HAVEN DRIVE (C7)

This street was dedicated as Dell Haven Drive on June 26, 1962. This street was originally dedicated on May 20, 1957, in Ordinance 107-57 as West 101st Street. However, the residents voted to change the name to Dell Haven, and it was changed on June 26, 1962. A dell is a secluded hollow or small valley or a "heavenly place of seclusion." Its residents claim that the numbered streets in this area were of little help to guiding people since they were off Reichert Road, a side street in the area. These streets were located behind Pleasant Valley Jr. High School. No one on the street could be found who knew why they picked this name. (See picture 50.)

DELLWOOD DRIVE (F4)

Dellwood Drive was dedicated on November 21, 1927. It was part of the Staten Heights Subdivision, which was an interesting subdivision of what is now Veterans' Memorial Park (formerly Petruska Park and State Road Park). (See plat map, page 57, and picture 39.) Dell means a secluded hollow or a small valley or a "wooded area of seclusion." It appears to be an aesthetically motivated name. Dellwood Drive has large tree lawns which add considerably to the appearance of the street. (See pictures 39 and 40.)

DENTZLER ROAD (Dentzer) (F6)

The name Dentzer goes back to the early history of Parma; it appears on an 1852 map. Two people by the name of H. and John Dentzer owned most of the land on the south side of today's Dentzler Road. The date of official dedication as far as can be researched was June 8, 1951. The road or drive to the Dentzer home existed long before this date. The Dentzer Family owned that land into the 1900's. As happens often, the spelling of names changes through the years, and this is what happened here.

DENVER DRIVE (B3)

Denver Drive was dedicated on June 19, 1967, in Ordinance 142-67. It is part of the Western Heights development. Slaben-MacKay were the developers. Appropriately enough, this development is located on the far west side of Parma, and the street names were of western cities.

DOGWOOD LANE (D7)

This street is part of the Dogwood Estates. Dogwood Lane was dedicated on November 7, 1962, in Ordinance 116-62. The dogwood tree was one of the many trees that "offered shelter, warmth and protection during the frontier days here in the Parma Area." This is quite an appropriate name for this street. I understand that there are 17 American species of dogwood trees. This street and others in the Dogwood Estates were named after trees, birds, nature areas and country locations; in general, this area has a very picturesque setting. Information is from *History of Parma*, by Ernest R. Kubasek, page 22, and City Hall records.

Early Plans for Residential Development for Veterans' Park
by
S. H. Kleinman and J. R. Taylor

Longwood Avenue

1997 Veterans' Park Pool

Entrances to
Veterans' Park 1997

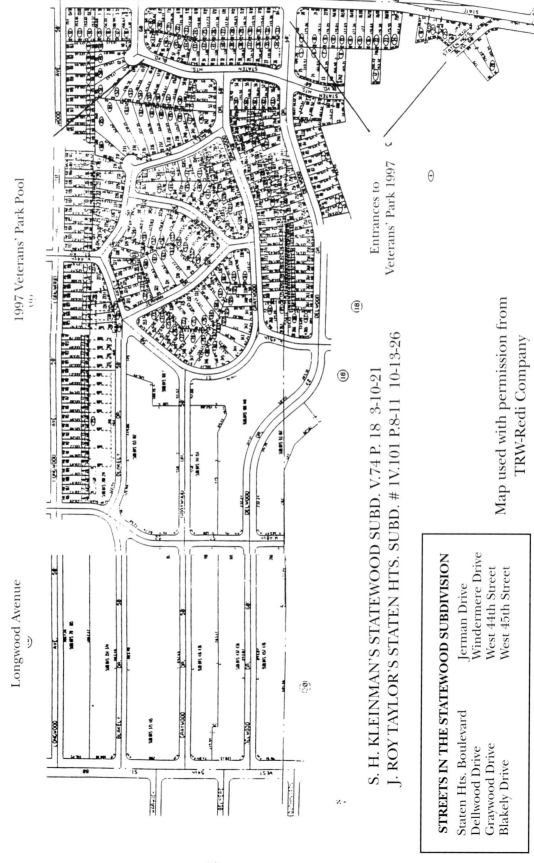

S. H. KLEINMAN'S STATEWOOD SUBD. V.74 P. 18 3-10-21
J. ROY TAYLOR'S STATEN HTS. SUBD. # IV.101 P.8-11 10-13-26

Map used with permission from
TRW-Redi Company

STREETS IN THE STATEWOOD SUBDIVISION

Staten Hts. Boulevard	Jerman Drive
Dellwood Drive	Windermere Drive
Graywood Drive	West 44th Street
Blakely Drive	West 45th Street

DONCASTER DRIVE (D4)

This street is part of the H. A. Stahl Development of Parma. It appears that H. A. Stahl applied the Garden City philosophy in Parma that the Van Sweringen brothers used in setting up Shaker Heights, including winding roads, lakes, and golf course. The street names were taken from Shaker Heights streets or taken from the same English source from which the Shaker Heights streets were named: the Garden Cities of England in the early 1900's. H. A. Stahl lived in Shaker Heights in the 1920's and had an office at Cedar and Coventry Roads. (See in this book "H. A. Stahl, A Tribute" for further information.) This street was dedicated by Parma Township officials on March 17, 1924. Doncaster is also a city in England located in South Yorkshire on the Don River. Information is from C. M. Matthews in her book *Place Names of the English Speaking World. Caster* comes from early Roman influence: "Ceaster" or "Castrall" means camp. Thus the translation of the street name is Camp by the River Don.

DOROTHY AVENUE (D3)

This street was dedicated on March 9, 1923. It appears to have been named after Dorothy Kelling. Dorothy and Barney Kelling owned this property from 1916 to 1925. This land was purchased from them by the developer, John Kobelt, on November 1, 1917. After extended research this appears to be a reasonably sound assumption. (See Bertha Avenue for further discussion.)

DOVER LANE (C7)

Dover Lane was dedicated on July 30, 1979, in Ordinance 143-79 at the request of the Broad-Beck Development Corporation. It was part of the Lake Estate Subdivision. Dover is one of the most used names in the naming of American cities; it was used sixteen times (*Place Names of the English speaking World* by C. M. Matthews). It is also used for parks. It is taken directly from the English. Recall Nat Burton's song "White Cliffs of Dover," from the 1940's. This song was probably a major catalyst in the naming of cities and streets. In this county alone, there are eight other streets by that name.

DRESDEN AVENUE (D2)

This street was part of the Tuxedo Lake Overlook Allotments. It was dedicated on April 4, 1924. The owners and developers were Arthur Hoffman, Oswald Kobelt, Werner Kobelt and Carrie Kobelt. They were all early settlers of Parma. They named this street and a number of others in this section of Parma after German cities, the so-called "German Estates." A number of the homes, colonials and bungalows, on Dresden Avenue were built in the 1920's and really give a good portrait of that period along with their unique fire station on the corner of Snow Road and Dresden Avenue. (See picture 33.) Dresden Avenue makes an interesting turn behind the fire station, as it turns on its way from Snow Road to Pearl Road, like something you might see in a German Village.

Streets and Roads . . . .

"I shall grow old, but never lose life's zest, Because the road's last turn will be the best."

Henry Van Dyke,
The Home Book of Quotations
by Burton Stevenson

E

EAST LINDEN LANE (A8)

East Linden Lane was dedicated on December 4, 1967, in Ordinance 409-67. It is part of a group of streets winding through the southwest corner of Parma. The area is very attractive, with large lots and country-like living. The land was owned by the H. M. Miller family and the H. L. Miller family. There were four streets: North, South, East and West Linden. Residents and former Mayor Day said these streets were named after the linden tree. In the development are also Millerwood Lane and Martin Drive. See the entries for these streets for further information.

EAST MIAMI DRIVE (F8)

East Miami Drive was dedicated on October 2, 1978 (City Ordinance 210-78). It was part of the "Florida Estates" located in the southern hills of Parma. It was during the 1960's and 1970's that these streets were laid out. It seems that Florida was becoming very popular to invest in, as people started becoming retirement-conscious, and Florida was a great place to retire. When former Mayor James Day was Councilman-at-large, during the 1960's, he, returning from a Florida vacation, suggested the Florida names. East Miami is actually not a suburb of Miami, Florida, but the name is probably given in relation to North Miami Drive, located in the same area in Parma.

EAST PARKVIEW DRIVE (G5-6)

East Parkview was dedicated on October 6. 1958, in Ordinance 281-58. If Don Helwick, an early developer in Parma, had his way, this street would probably be called South Park Boulevard East. He seems to have had plans to run South Park Boulevard East and South Park Boulevard West, south from Broadview to Grantwood Drive or possibly to Pleasant Valley Road with the Quarry Creek Park between them. This is the area where East Parkview Drive is located. It seems that only the Depression of the 1930's stopped him

from pursuing this plan. This street was then developed by the Pentz Builders in 1958.

EDGECLIFF DRIVE (G6)

Edgecliff Drive runs around the top of a cliff in a semicircle at the end of Augustine Drive. The backyards of many of the homes on this street have wooded areas that drop off into a valley which is part of the Quarry Creek system. This is a very appropriate name for this street. Edgecliff was dedicated on December 1, 1964, in Ordinance 270-64.

EDGEHILL DRIVE (C2)

Edgehill Drive (in Parma) was dedicated on December 4, 1939, in Resolution 53-39. This street is the continuation of a street in Parma Heights dedicated on February 5, 1924. It is continued into the Greenbriar Estates, which was a very exclusive area of Parma in the 1940's. In Parma Heights, this street, in part, runs along the top of the hill that is part of Big Creek Parkway, which might account for how this street received its name. However, it is also believed that it got its name from Cleveland Heights. It seems that many of the streets in Parma received their names from Cleveland Heights and Shaker Heights during this period. Edgehill Road in Cleveland Heights runs off Washington Boulevard, south of Lakeview Cemetery. The naming of these streets epitomized the Garden City philosophy of the developers during the 1920's. (See "H. A. Stahl, A Tribute" in this book.) (See picture 53.)

ELDON DRIVE (C2) (C3 Parma Heights)

Eldon Drive was dedicated in Parma Heights on January 2, 1925. Eldon Drive started in Parma Heights and ran into a very exclusive area of Parma at the time and still is. This street is also believed to have been named with the Garden City philosophy in mind, in which most of the street names came from England. In London there is a street named Eldon Street. The street in London was named after John Scott, the Earl of Eldon (1821). Prior to that he was Lord

Chancellor in 1801. He was also Governor of the Charterhouse and was a trustee of the British Museum. (Information is from *City of London Streets* by Al Smith. See Parkland Drive for further information and see also "H. A. Stahl, A Tribute." (See picture 53.)

ELIZABETH AVENUE (C2)

Elizabeth Avenue was dedicated on September 27, 1954, in ordinance 198-54. According to Sam Miller's office, this street was named after Sam Miller's sister, Elizabeth Miller. At the intersections of Elizabeth Avenue and Gabriella Drive and Elizabeth Avenue and Deborah Drive, there are large triangular traffic islands which give an attractive park-like appearance to the neighborhood. The streets connected at angles create interesting property lines.

ELSMERE DRIVE (C2)

Elsmere Drive is part of the Greenbriar Estate, which had been a very exclusive community during the mid 1900's. It was dedicated on December 4, 1939, in Resolution 53-39. Doctors and lawyers were residents in this community at that time. All the streets in Greenbriar were named after streets in Shaker Heights. The idea of Parma being for a high-class, exclusive community was continued in this development. For further information see Parkland Drive and also "H. A. Stahl, A Tribute." (See picture 53.)

ELY VISTA DRIVE (D6)

The Justine Ely Family had acquired land (Ely Tract) in the Western Reserve land tract located just south of where Parmatown is now located. They had this land on paper when the first settlers, the Fay family, settled in Parma in 1816. Ely Vista Drive is located just south of Parma's Historic Stearns Farm, which is in about the middle of the Ely Tract. It took about 175 years before the name Ely was given to some physical location in Parma. Ely Vista Drive was dedicated on July 16, 1979, in Ordinance 105-79.

ENDERBY DRIVE (C2)

Enderby Drive is part of the Greenbriar Estates, an exclusive community in the 1940's, 1950's and 1960's. Enderby Drive was dedicated on December 4, 1939. This was a community of large brick homes; some of them could be described as mansions. Wealthy people lived in this community, many doctors and lawyers. You had to be approved by the Greenbriar Board of Directors before moving into Greenbriar. The rules governing this development were dropped in 1973. There is also an Enderby Road in Shaker Heights, a Garden City. (For further information, see Parkland Drive.) (See picture 53.)

ENGLEWOOD DRIVE (G3)

Bertha Engel was the owner of the property on which this street was laid out. The name has been misspelled and may even be misspelled on street signs as it is on maps. It is speculation to say this street was named after Bertha Engel, but a plausible one, inasmuch as streets are often named after the property owners. Engelwood Drive was dedicated as a street on June 28, 1926, by City Council Ordinance 290 under the name of Englewood. The street is located one block south of Rockside Road, east off Broadview Road.

ESPER AVENUE (G6)

Esper Avenue was named after Adoph and Daisy Esper. They were Laverne Esper Hunter's grandparents. The Esper family owned property off State Road in this area in the early 1900's; in fact, the brick home they lived in is still standing on State Road. Laverne Esper Hunter was 75 years old at the time of our conversation (10-7-89). Esper Avenue was dedicated as part of the Chestnut Heights Allotment on October 6, 1924. (Information is from Cuyahoga Plat Maps and Laverne Esper Hunter.)

ESSEN AVENUE (D3)

Essen Avenue is part of the Tuxedo Orchard Allotments. Though not part of what you might call the "German Estates" (Tuxedo Lake Overlook Allotments), it is located in the same area. Essen is a name of a large city in Germany located near Cologne. Essen Avenue is located just south of Snow Road between Pearl and Ridge Roads. Immediately to the north of Snow are the so-called German Allotments. Here, streets were given names of German cities. The same developers were involved, Freida and John Kobelt. Essen Avenue was dedicated on March 3, 1923.

EVANS DRIVE (B8)

After extensive research over a couple of years, no one, from the residents on the street to public officials, could give any reason why this street was named Evans Drive. The only notable person in Ernie Kubasek's *History of Parma* named Evans was Lewis Evans, the man who made the first accurate map of the Ohio area in 1755. The name of the street was changed to Evans Drive by City Council on October 4, 1965 (Ordinance 212-65). However, no city official could give any reason why it was named Evans Drive. Originally it was named West 108th Street on February 3, 1964 (Ordinance 26-64).

EVENTIDE DRIVE (D6)

Eventide Drive was dedicated on July 16, 1979, in Ordinance 105-79. It was named by the Sunrise Builders, which might give a hint as to why this street was named as such. In this very neat development, some of the most attractive names were used, such as Night Vista Drive, Dawn Vista Oval, Mooncrest Drive and Sun Vista. All of these names seem to be related to the name "Sunrise Builders."

EVERGREEN DRIVE (C2)

Evergreen Drive was originally dedicated as Tuxedo Lake Road on August 28, 1919. Frank Johnson, owner of the land, named the Tuxedo Lake and Tuxedo Lake Road. Residents say he is also the one who planted

hundreds of evergreen trees all through the development. It was because of these evergreen trees, which grew up into a beautiful wooded area, that the residents changed the name of the lake and the street to Evergreen Lake and Evergreen Drive on May 31, 1927, in Ordinance 508. Other members of the Johnson Family involved as owners were Julia F. Johnson, John F. Johnson, and Belle Johnson.

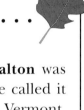

Did you know that . . . .

The City of **North Royalton** was named by Knight Sprague. He called it after his hometown of Royalton, Vermont. He was one of four founders of this city. The others were John Coates, Robert Engle, and David Sprague. Names sound familiar?

The City of **North Randall** was named after Postmaster General Alexander W. Randall. It was named after him when the Post Office was established in 1868. North Randall was incorporated in 1908.

The City of **Avon** was originally known as Xeuma and later as Troy. It eventually took the name of the Township in 1824. The township was named after Avon, Massachusetts.

OHIO PLACE NAMES by Larry L. Miller
University of Indiana Press, 1996

FAIRLAWN DRIVE (B2)

This street was dedicated on August 22, 1960, in City Ordinance 166-60. Some of the first homes on the street were built by Selby Homes, a builder in Cleveland in the late 1930's and early 1940's. This street appears to be named aesthetically. Could it have been named because of its geographic location, a park setting? The east end of the street terminates at Hauserman Road, which borders the Big Creek Park.

FARNSWORTH DRIVE (D4)

This street was dedicated on November 23, 1921, at the request of H. A. Stahl, who named most of the streets he laid out at the Parma Circle location. It appears that H. A. Stahl applied many of the ideas in Parma that were used in setting up Shaker Heights, Ohio, collectively known as the Garden City philosophy. Included were winding roads, lakes, and a golf course. The street names were taken from Shaker Heights streets or taken from the same English sources from which the Shaker Heights streets were named, the Garden Cities of England of the 1920's. H. A. Stahl lived in Shaker Heights in the 1920's and had an office at Cedar and Coventry Roads. (See in this book "H. A. Stahl, A Tribute" for further information.) There is a place in England called Farnworth. "Farn" means ferns covering a field and "Worth" would probably be a name of a family. Information is from *Place Names of the English Speaking World* by C.M. Matthews, page 65.

FATIMA DRIVE (G6)

Fatima Drive is located in the Broadview/Gettysburg Estate area. This street was developed by Albert Rispo Realty and Development Company. Mr. Rispo named this street after the town in Portugal where the Blessed Virgin appeared to three young children in 1917. Many cures have been credited to these appearances, and she is said to have made predictions about world politics. Fatima Drive was dedicated on October 10, 1989, in Ordinance 324-89.

FAY DRIVE (G7)

Fay Drive was named after the first settlers in Parma, the Benajah Fay family. They settled in 1816 near what is today the Pearl/Ridge Road intersection. This street was dedicated to them on April 21, 1975, in Ordinance 25-75, 159 years after the first settlement. Doctor Dudley Fay, before he died on January 16, 1992, was very helpful to this author with his knowledge of the early days of Parma. Dr. Fay was born on March 26, 1906. Ruth Fay, his daughter, a retired Parma teacher, was also helpful. (Information is from Parma City Ordinance 25-75.)

FENWAY DRIVE (D6)

Fenway Drive was dedicated on May 20, 1957, in Ordinance 113-57. It was named after a University Circle hotel, Fenway Hotel. It seems it was an ideal place for a business meeting, a place where developers would hold their meetings in the 1950's. It was called Fenway Hall. Businessman and developer George Seltzer is the one who named this street. Information is from Mr. Leonard Lane, who through marriage was acquainted with George Seltzer.

FERNHILL AVENUE (C2)

Fernhill Avenue is located in the northwest section of Parma. One resident said that the street rises on a hill, and he believes that there were fern–like trees on the street. He thought that is how the street got its name. This street also runs right into the Big Creek Parkway. It is in quite an attractive setting. Fernhill Avenue was dedicated on April 2, 1917. The land owner was John P. Teufel, and the developer was S. H. Kleinman Realty. The subdivision was called the Forest Lawn Subdivision.

FLEGER DRIVE (F8)

This street was named after Anthony Fleger, Parma's first Democratic mayor. He was elected on November 3, 1933, and left office in 1935. Fleger Drive was dedicated on May 7, 1973, in Ordinance 34-73, thirty-eight years after the mayor left office. Information is from *History of Parma* by Ernest R. Kubasek and from former Mayor James Day.

FORDHAM DRIVE (E4)

Fordham Drive was dedicated on March 23, 1959, in Ordinance 53-59. It was part of the "Ridgewood Subdivision." Par Homes were the developers. Fordham University is located in New York City, and in all probability, the street was named after this university. It is a Jesuit university. The other street in this two-street development is Loyola Drive, named for another Jesuit university in Chicago. Living associates of the developers did not know for sure why the streets were given these names.

FOREST AVENUE (D2)

Forest Avenue was dedicated on September 13, 1919. It was part of the Ridgewood Garden Allotment. According to an early resident, this street was a wooded area and the street might have received its name from its location. However, H. A. Stahl was Secretary for the Wooster Park Land Company when the original dedication took place. Later Mr. Stahl had another part of the street dedicated on April 29, 1920, under the H. A. Stahl Properties Company. Forest Avenue was the start of Mr. Stahl's effort to organize Parma Circle (Ridgewood Circle) into a very attractive community. There are twenty streets in Cuyahoga County named Forest and 41 more that have "Forest" in their name. This area was known for its beautiful trees, and the name surely reflects this. (See "H. A. Stahl, A Tribute.")

FOREST HILLS BOULEVARD (E5)

Forest Hills Boulevard was originally called Chestnut Hills Boulevard. It was changed on May 16, 1932 (Ordinance 55), to Forest Hills Boulevard because there was another street in the city with the same name. Forest Hills Boulevard is quite an appropriate name since the street runs along a cliff overlooking the

wooded area of Ridgewood Drive. The residents on the north side of the street truly have an excellent view of the woods and, in the winter, a view of northern Parma, Cleveland and Lake Erie. It is like having a lodge on the hills overlooking the Cuyahoga County low lands and Lake Erie. It is a truly an excellent view of God's creation.

FT. MYERS DRIVE (F8)

Ft. Myers Drive was dedicated on October 8, 1987, in Ordinance 183-87. It is part of the second group of streets named after Florida cities. The city is located on Florida's west coast. It all started when Councilman-at-large, soon to be elected Mayor, James Day returned from a vacation in Florida and thought naming the streets after Florida cities would be attractive. This was in 1961, when the first group of streets received their names. (See Winter Park Drive for more information.)

FORTUNE AVENUE (F2)

Fortune Avenue was dedicated on October 23, 1915. It was part of the State Park Allotment. The owner of the land at that time was Retta Laronge. It is not clear why the name Fortune was used, but there could be many good reasons in one's personal life that might warrant the name "Fortune." Fortune Avenue is a popular street on Cleveland's northwest side also.

FOX HOLLOW DRIVE (C7)

Fox Hollow Drive was dedicated on July 7, 1980, in Ordinance 114-79. It is a street located off York Road, one street north of Pleasant Lake Boulevard, in a very natural area. It leads into a group of streets called the Black Forest Acres, a community of winding roads over a hilly countryside. You could almost see where a fox could be hiding in a hollow on the hillside. These streets and other streets in the area are located near the German Central Farm, hence the Black Forest name. Information is from Ordinance 114-79 at City Hall.

FRANKFORT AVENUE (D3)

This street would seem to be named after Frankfurt, Germany, in spite of the spelling. It is in a development in which all the streets are named after German cities. In this country in other locations the name is spelled Frankfort, as in Frankfort, Kentucky. It was part of the Tuxedo Lake Overlook Allotments. Frankfort Avenue was dedicated on April 21, 1924. The developers were Arthur Hoffman, Oswald Kobelt, Werner Kobelt and Carrie Kobelt. Robert Hoffman was the Chief Engineer for the group. (Information is from County office, Room 216, Vol. 89, page 20.)

FREEHOLD ROAD (Fl)

Freehold Road is the first street south of Brookpark Road off State Road. It is very short and runs into Daleside Drive and into a very attractive area. It is part of the "Henninger/ Uhinck" development. Freehold Road was dedicated on April 20, 1918. This was immediately after the First World War. Like many streets, could this street have been named after the concerns people had at that time?

FRIAR DRIVE (F7)

This street is part of the "Robinhood Estates." It runs between Marko Lane and Ward Road. The Friar is a character in the Robinhood tales; the street might have been named in reference to this character in the tales of Robinhood. Friar Drive was dedicated on July 5, 1960 (Ordinance 130-60). This was part of the Gulfedge Subdivision #2.

FRUITLAND DRIVE (E5)

Fruitland Drive was dedicated on January 2, 1923. It was part of the Highland Orchard Development by developers Elworth and Helwick. Jim Corson, who has lived in this area since the street was built and who now lives on Fruitland Drive, said this street and Orchard Park Drive were named as such because they were developed at the site of a large orchard.

GABRIELLA DRIVE (B2)

Gabriella Drive was dedicated on September 20, 1954. The street was named after Gabriella Miller, one of Sam Miller's children. Sam Miller was the developer for the Forest City Enterprises. Gabriella Drive rises up to a knoll and gives an exceptional view of the neighborhood. (Information was from the City Engineer's office and Sam Miller's office.)

GEORGE AVENUE (F3)

This street was named after the George Family. Habeeb George and Shaheen George were early (1920's) residents of the Village of Parma. These two brothers formed a construction company called the George Brothers Construction Company. It was a sewer construction company. They did quite a bit of work around Parma. They also bought some land, and set up George Avenue. They were assisted by two more members of the family, Minor and Rudy George, in building homes on the street. George Avenue was dedicated on April 15, 1927. (Information is from *History of Parma*, by Ernie Kubasek.)

GERALD AVENUE (D2)

This street was named after Gerald Fitzgerald, uncle to developer Gordon Reichwein. He was a realtor during the 1920's. The street was dedicated on April 29, 1920, in the Ridgewood Garden Allotment.

GETTYSBURG DRIVE (G6)

Gettysburg Drive was named after the Battle of Gettysburg by Mayor James Day after he returned from a trip to Gettysburg. It is part of the "Gettysburg Estates." It was dedicated on December 2, 1968, in Ordinance 396-68 as part of the Charles Subdivision #2.

GILBERT AVENUE (D2)

Gilbert Avenue was dedicated on April 29, 1920, and was part of the Ridgewood Garden Allotments. H. A. Stahl was the developer.

Extensive research has been done on Gilbert Avenue, but no viable answer as to whom this street was named after could be found, until a letter was received from a Virginia Fox Brown of Tampa, Florida, on April 25, 1997. In her letter she states that Gilbert Avenue was named after her brother Gilbert Brown (1910-1987), the son of Thomas B. Brown, who was Sales Director for the H. A. Stahl Company. Gilbert Brown was in construction most of his life.

GLAMER DRIVE (B7)

Any similarity between Glamer, as in Glamer Drive, and glamour, as in beauty, is purely coincidental. Why? Because, according to Toni Dietz, Barney Glansbeek (Toni's father) and a friend, a Mr. Shermer, got together and decided to name a street in their development "Glamer Drive." You see, Barney took the first three letters in his name GLA and the last three letters in his friend's name MER and put them together to spell Glamer Drive. Barney Glansbeek and his family were early land owners in the area of Glamer Drive. Glamer Drive runs west off York Road, two blocks south of Pleasant Valley Road. Glamer Drive was dedicated on April 15, 1957, in Ordinance 63-57. (Information was received from former Mayor James Day and Toni Dietz.)

GLENN DRIVE (Glen) (F4)

This street was not named after John Glenn, the astronaut inasmuch as it was named before he was well known. The street was dedicated on October 7, 1957, by City Council Ordinance 250-57. Research has not uncovered any leads as to whom this street might be named after. Research is still being carried out. If anyone has information on the naming of this street, please call the Historical Society.

GLENCAIRN DRIVE (G6)

This street was developed by two Scotsmen, Don and Robert MacDonald. They gave this street the name Glencairn. It is a Scottish word which means a valley near a river. This is exactly where this street is located in the Quarry Creek Valley area. It is an outstanding nature area with a large valley behind the homes on the east side of the street overlooking the Quarry Creek Valley. Glencairn Drive was dedicated on July 16, 1956, in Ordinance 156-56.

GLENN OVAL DRIVE (C7)

This street was renamed by the residents on June 26, 1962, in Ordinance 79-62. They named this street after John Glenn, the astronaut and future senator. The street was formerly dedicated on May 20, 1957, in Ordinance 107-57 as West 91st Street. Mr. Glenn, being an Ohio resident, made this renaming quite appropriate. According to one resident, all the streets in this area that were numbered streets were supposed to be named after astronauts. Somehow it never worked out that way. (See picture 50.)

GOEBEL DRIVE (G4)

Some residents may remember Joseph Goebel, who was a councilman during the 1950's. You may also remember that he was the prime mover in the creation of State Road Park. He retired in 1963 at the age of 76 after serving 19 years on City Council. The street was dedicated on July 20, 1970, in Ordinance 232-70. Goebel Drive runs parallel to Ridgewood Drive (up on the cliff overlooking Quarry Creek) between Broadview and State Roads. This information was secured from records at Parma City Hall and Leo Hepner, a long-time resident who was active in Parma politics in the 1950's.

GORDON DRIVE (B7)

Gordon Drive was dedicated on October 4, 1965, in Ordinance 199-65. It was named after Gordon Reichwein, who was one of the developers in this area. Richard MacKay was the engineer. This was called the Richard Subdivision.

GRANT DRIVE (G6)

Grant Drive was named after Union General in the Civil War, and later eighteenth president, Ulysses S. Grant. The street was dedicated on

December 2, 1968, in Ordinance 396-68. Though this is generally known as the Gettysburg Estates it was dedicated on the above date as the Charles Subdivision #2. The name was suggested by Mayor James Day after he returned from his vacation at Gettysburg.

GRANTWOOD DRIVE (E4)

Grantwood Drive was originally given the name of Wick Road. This name, historically speaking, was most appropriate for the street. In 1903 a man by the name of J. P. Wick owned the land from State Road to Quarry Creek (the creek between State and Broadview Roads) along the south side of the present Grantwood Drive. Grantwood was dedicated as Wick Road on March 23, 1923, and changed to Grantwood Drive on November 9, 1925. It seems the Grantwood Realty Company developed a group of houses on Wick Road called the Grantwood Heights Subdivision around 1922, but the name wasn't changed to Grantwood until 1925. There was also a property owner named A. A. Wick who owned land in the Parmadale area. (See pictures 39, 46 and 49.)

GREEN ACRES DRIVE (G8)

During the time of research on this street many of the residents asked if this street had been named after the 1960 television program *Green Acres*. That is a possibility, but I think it must be taken into account that this street is located in the area of the Green Valley Estates, and that may have been a catalyst in naming this street Green Acres Drive. Green Acres Drive was dedicated on December 17, 1962, in Ordinance 164-62. It was part of the Pleasant Acres Estates.

GREEN VALLEY DRIVE (G8)

Green Valley Drive was dedicated on December 7, 1959 (Ordinance 213-59), at the request of Homestead Builders. The street probably received its name from its location in a valley of trees through which Pleasant Valley Road runs. At that time Pleasant Valley Road was a two-lane

road, and it was very impressive as it passed from Broadview Road west into a broad valley of trees to the State Road area. Green Valley Drive is located south off Pleasant Valley Road between Broadview and State Roads. (Information is from a table of Special Ordinances of the City of Parma.)

GREENLAWN AVENUE (DRIVE) (D2)

Greenlawn Avenue was part of the Lake Park Allotment. The land owners were Catherine and Frank Bauer, and they developed this land and apparently named the streets. This development included Bauerdale Drive. There are many trees in this area that form a very natural park setting; this may be the reason for this street being called Greenlawn. It is also located near Evergreen Lake. Evergreen Drive is another street in this heavily wooded area. Greenlawn Avenue was dedicated on April 13, 1923.

GREENLEAF AVENUE (A7)

This street was dedicated on May 6, 1929, and was part of the Briar Cliff Subdivision. It is located in the southwest section of Parma off Pleasant Valley Road and continues into Parma Heights; it terminates at Pearl Road. There were many trees in the area which might have been a factor in the naming of this street.

GROSS DRIVE (B8)

This street was named after Marvin Gross, who was a builder and developer (especially of this street). This street was dedicated on February 20, 1961, in Ordinance 26-61 (Information is from County Plat Book 194, page 63, and former Mayor James Day.)

GROVEWOOD AVENUE (F2)

Grovewood Avenue was originally dedicated as Boston Avenue on April 28, 1922 (Plat Vol. 81, page 15). On June 14, 1926, part of the street name was changed by City Council to Grovewood. On March 7, 1938, the complete street was changed to Grovewood in City Ordinance 7. It is not at this time clear why the name was changed. There is a good chance that an orchard grove was located in this area from which the street received its name. Ettie Moran was the developer and the one who laid out Tuxedo Avenue and other streets in the Brooklyn Heights–Parma area. (See picture 45.)

GUADELOUPE DRIVE (H6)

This street is located off Broadview Road, just north of the Gettysburg Estates. Guadeloupe Drive was developed by Albert Rispo Realty and Development Company. Mr. Rispo named this street after the town in Mexico where the Blessed Virgin, on December 9, 1531, is said to have appeared to a young man by the name of Juan Diego. A shrine was built there, and Our Lady of Guadeloupe became the patroness of Mexico. This street was dedicated on May 11, 1992, in Ordinance 303-91.

Did you know that . . . .

The City of **Elyria** was named after Herman Ely. He donated the land and money for the seat of the county Government. Does that name mean something to Parma? See *The History of Parma* by Ernest R. Kubasek, page 72.

The City of **Mansfield** was established in 1808 and was named after Jared Mansfield, a surveyor for the United States Government.

Lordstown in Trumbull County was named after Samuel P. Lord. It was not incorporated until 1975.

OHIO PLACE NAMES by Larry L. Miller
University of Indiana Press, 1996

HACIENDA DRIVE (C7)

Hacienda Drive has had two names. It was originally dedicated in 1957 as West 94th Street. On June 26, 1962, the residents had the name changed to Hacienda Drive in Ordinance 79-62. No resident could be found who knew why they picked Hacienda for their name. In the 1950's there were a number of popular songs about Central America on the *Hit Parade*. Central America was presented as a romantic place in songs. A couple of songs were "In My Adobe Hacienda" and "Managua, Nicaragua, Is a Beautiful Place." The catalyst in naming this street might have been the above songs. Hacienda means house or home in Spanish. This is quite a nice name for a street where the homes of many people are located.

HAMPSTEAD AVENUE
(Hampsted Avenue) (D3)

Hampstead Avenue was part of the H. A. Stahl layout of Ridgewood Circle. Most of Mr. Stahl's Streets were named after English place names, and this one is no exception. There is a section in Greater London called Hampstead. It is located on a subway line in the north central part of the city. The word *Homestead* means the same as *Hampstead*. *Ham* means place of living and *stede* or *stead* means place. Another street in Parma had the name Homestead at one time but was changed, and it became Thorton Drive. The change we understand was to prevent confusion between Homestead and Hampstead. This street was dedicated Hampstead Avenue on June 30, 1921, at the request of H. A. Stahl. (For further information see "H. A. Stahl, A Tribute" in this book.) (See picture 22.)

HAROLD AVENUE (B7)

Harold Avenue was dedicated on October 3, 1955, in Ordinance 239-55. The street was named after Harold Bejcek, who was Parma's Solicitor from 1954 to 1960. Information was received from Ed Demeter, a builder who

- 67 -

worked for the city of Parma for many years. Mr. Demeter was president of the K-D Construction Company in Parma during the 1950's.

HARROW DRIVE (C2)

Harrow Drive, along with a number of other streets in this development located in the north central part of Parma, was named after an English institution of learning. Harrow is an independent boarding school housing approximately 775 boys situated about 10 miles from London. The school was founded in 1572 under a Royal charter granted by Elizabeth I. Evidence for this creditable assumption is that other streets in this same neighborhood were named after elite English and American schools, such as Roedean Drive, Cambridge Drive, Dartmouth Drive, Kenyon Drive, and Amherst Drive. This street was dedicated on November 6, 1961, in city Ordinance 200-61 (See Roedean Drive for further information.)

HARWOOD DRIVE (A6)

Harwood Drive was dedicated on October 7, 1957, in Ordinance 249-57. This is a cross street from Maplewood Road to Beresford Avenue. Harwood Drive is located on the southern boundary of Parma Heights and Parma. No one connected with the developer could give a reason for naming this street Harwood. This is truly an English name as there are places in Lancashire, Northumberland, and West Yorkshire with this name. Research is still being carried out on this street. If anyone knows anything about the naming of this street, please call the Parma Historical Society.

HAUSERMAN ROAD (C2)

Actually, much of the Hauserman land at one time belonged to the family of John Snell. When his daughter Angeline married John (Frederick) Hauserman (May 29, 1850), her father gave her a large section of this property, and it eventually became known as the Hauserman Farm. Angeline's mother was Nancy (Thumb) Snell.

The Hauserman name was given to the road (which was Hauserman's driveway off Brookpark road) between 1851 and 1874. Hauserman Road borders the wooded area of the Metroparks on the south end. Hauserman Road was named after the John (Frederick) Hauserman family (also spelled Hausserman). Information is from Martin Hauserman, great grandson of John (Frederick) Hauserman. The first official dedication date that can be determined is April 21, 1958, in city Ordinance 111-58. (See picture 53.)

HAVERHILL AVENUE (E3)

Haverhill Avenue was dedicated on November 23, 1921. It was part of the Ridgewood Estates #4. This street is part of the H. A. Stahl Development. It appears that H. A. Stahl applied all the ideas in Parma that were used in setting up Shaker Heights; these ideas constitute the Garden City philosophy. Incorporated were winding roads, lakes, and a golf course. The street names were taken from Shaker Heights streets or taken from the same English source from which the Shaker Heights streets were named, the Garden Cities of England in the 1920's. H. A. Stahl lived in Shaker Heights in the 1920's and had an office at Cedar and Coventry Roads. There is a town in England about 25 miles northeast of London that has the name of Haverhill. (See in this book "H. A. Stahl, A Tribute" for further discussion.)

HAWTHORNE CIRCLE (F4)

This street was dedicated on October 7, 1968, in city Ordinance 422-67. Hawthorne Circle is almost a continuation of Hawthorne Drive. It quite obviously took its name from Hawthorne Drive. Hawthorne Drive (a private road) was named by Mayor James Day's sister, Eleanor Haendiges, who lived in the only house on the street. The street, Hawthorne Drive, it is believed, received its name from the Hawthorne Dominican Nuns, the nuns who run the Holy Family Cancer Home. See Hawthorne Drive for further information.

HAWTHORNE DRIVE (Private) (F5)

Hawthorne Drive (a private road) was named by Mayor James Day's sister, Eleanor Haendiges, who lived in the only house on the street. The street, it is believed, received its name from the Hawthorne Dominican Nuns, the nuns who run the Holy Family Cancer Home. This street and the land around it was owned by the Day Family when Ridgewood Drive was called Valley View Road. Eleanor Haendiges lived in the house on this street until it was destroyed in 1996. It is now a back road leading to Parmadale's Children's Village (See Hawthorne Circle above for more information.)

HEARTHSTONE ROAD (F2)

Hearthstone Road was dedicated on August 8, 1925, by the Hearthstone Land Company. The developers were H. D. McCollough (also spelled McCullough) and W. L. Cook (Treasurer). There is a feeling that the Hearthstone Road was part of the Garden City development, as were other streets in this development: Sedgwick Avenue, Malverne Avenue, South Park Boulevard and Torrington Avenue. All these street names can be found in Shaker Heights, Ohio, a prime example of a Garden City. It seems they could have been working with Donald Helwick, who was a developer in the area. (See "Don Helwick, A Man With a Plan" in this book.) The present day Hearthstone Development Company is unrelated to the Hearthstone Land Company of 1927.

HERESFORD DRIVE (F3)

This street was dedicated on March 23, 1923. The developers were Aberdeen Park Allotments by Elworthy and Helwick. It seems that during this time a number of streets were named after English place names. H. A. Stahl, who laid out Parma Circle, used English places extensively. This again was in the early 1920's. Hereford (Herefordshire) is a county in England just southwest of Birmingham, England. However, there is no "s" in the English county name; it is not known what happened to the "s" in the English county name. There is also a street in Cleveland Heights by the name of Hereford Road, near where Mr. Helwick lived. This again could be part of the Garden City concept. Hereford is the name of a type of beef cattle named after Hereford, England, where cattle of this type were raised. (See picture 46.)

HETZEL DRIVE (F6)

This street was named after Mary Hetzel, who was a councilwoman from 1946 to 1960. She also ran a florist shop on State Road. Her floral shop was located next to Kader Appliance Store, which is located at Grovewood and State Road. Hetzel Drive was dedicated as part of the Rolling Acres Subdivision on November 3, 1958, in Ordinance 303-58.

HIALEAH DRIVE (E8)

Hialeah Drive was dedicated on May 5, 1975, in Ordinance 90-75. It is one of the streets in the second "Florida Estates." It is located in the Sarasota Drive and State Road area. Hialeah is a suburb of Miami, Florida. Most people know this suburb because of the race track that is located in it. See Winterpark Drive for a further explanation on this street.

HICKORY HILL LANE (C8)

Hickory Hill Lane is located in the Dogwood Estates. The name Hickory comes from a family of North American hardwood walnut trees. They often have sweet edible nuts. It is thought that this tree had such hard wood that it was used for punishing a child (whipping). However, I am sure that this street was named in reference to a hill of walnut trees giving abundant shade in the summer for picnics and parties. Hickory Hill Lane was dedicated on November 20, 1967, in Ordinance 421-67.

HIDDEN VALLEY CIRCLE (D7)

Hidden Valley Circle is part of the Hidden Valley Drive Development (Dogwood Estates Development). It was dedicated on June 4, 1979, in Ordinance 16-79. This whole development is in proximity of the Original (1968) Dogwood Estates off Pleasant Valley Road but is not physically connected. For further information on this street see Hidden Valley Lane below.

HIDDEN VALLEY LANE (D7)

Hidden Valley Lane was dedicated on June 4, 1979, in Ordinance 16-79. It was part of the Dogwood Estates Development. This street is in a very attractive area, and the name fits the street well. It is located in a valley south of Pleasant Valley Road off Ridge Road. It is somewhat hidden from the public eye. Though this street is not connected with the Dogwood Estates either in time or location, it is part of the development.

HIGHLAND HILLS COURT (D8)

Highland Hills Court is part of the Pine Tree Development. It is located north of Sprague Road between Ridge Road and York Road. This street and others in this development were named after golf courses. Highland Park Golf Course (slight change in name) is located in Warrensville Heights. Richard MacKay, the developer, tells us that an oak tree on this property, believed to be over two hundred years old, has been identified with a plaque. It has been named the Moses Oak after Moses Cleaveland, as it was discovered during the 200th Anniversary year of his landing on the banks of the Cuyahoga River. Highland Hills Court was dedicated on January 17, 1994, in Ordinance 209-94.

HIGHVIEW DRIVE (D6)

Highview Drive was dedicated on November 3, 1965, in Ordinance 235-65. It is a very neat but short street that terminates in an area overlooking a small valley, which might be the

reason for its name. Part of this street was renamed Lime Lane in 1992. It was part of the Sidney Simon Subdivision #1.

HILLCREST LANE (G7)

Hillcrest Lane is located in the Broad-Valle Subdivision and extends into the Green Valley Subdivision. There is a Hillcrest Country Club in Miami, Florida. Since most of these streets are named after Florida locations, this might be the reason for the name. However, south of the street is a hill which is one of the highest points in Cuyahoga county. This might also be the reason for the name. Part of Hillcrest Lane was dedicated on December 21, 1959 (Green Valley Estates), and part was dedicated on April 17, 1961 (Broad Valle Subdivision, Ordinance 225-59).

HILLSDALE AVENUE (G3)

Hillsdale Avenue is located in the vicinity of "Quarry Creek Valley" and Broadview Road near Broadview and Snow Roads. This street was dedicated on March 21, 1927, at the request of the K & L Land company. R. C. Johnson and Jack Lampl were the owners. It seems this street might have received its name from its location. Every other street in this area seems to be named based on its location. Hillsdale Avenue is located not too far from the Broadview Road hill that goes into the Quarry Creek. At the time of the dedication of this street, this might have been a very pronounced view (see Meadowlawn Boulevard). Research has not been able to come up with any other positive reasons behind the naming of the street. Information on the dedication is from the County Plat Book 105, page 38.

HILLTOP DRIVE (F6)

Hilltop Drive was dedicated on April 15, 1957, in Ordinance 80-57 and County Plat Volume 165, page 34. According to Anthony Deroia, a 91-year-old resident, Hilltop Drive got its name from Hilltop Tavern, which was located in that area before the street. This street is located about one mile from State Road hill and overlooks the city of Cleveland. Mr. William Hoislbauer II, the developer, said the Hilltop Riding Academy was located just to the north of Hilltop Road and the Tavern was just in front of it. He says he believes the road got its name from the Hilltop Tavern and Riding Academy. The Tavern burned down in the early 1950's, and that is when the "Three Bills Ink Corporation" bought up the land. The three Bills were William Hoislbauer, the first, second and third. William Circle off Rustic Trail was named after William Hoislbauer III, a child at the time.

HOERTZ ROAD (F8)

This street was named after the J. M. Hoertz family. John Hoertz owned property from Hoertz to Broadview Road. His son William Hoertz, who died in 1978, owned the property after him. The property was sold sometime in the 1940's. William's wife, Barbara, died on July 1, 1996, at the age of 86, just before we contacted the Hoertz family. Karen Robison was our informant; she is the wife of Mark Robison, who is the stepson of William Hoertz, Barbara's husband. Hoertz Road was not dedicated until March 19, 1956, in Ordinance 59-56. Initial information is from the 1903 County Property Map.

HOLBURN ROAD (D4)

Holburn Road was dedicated on December 12, 1923 (Plat Map Vol. 85, page 8). This street is part of the H. A. Stahl Development. It appears H. A. Stahl took the name of this street from the same source from which he took the other street names in his Ridgewood Circle Development: the Garden City maps or directories of England. Holborn or Hol-burne was the name given to that part of the old "River Fleet" that flowed under Holborn Viaduct in London. Holborn, then, is really the burne or river in the hollow, the hollow being the valley at the eastern end of Holborn, which was spanned by the Holborn Viaduct. This is a very historic place in London. (Information is from the *Dictionary of City of London Street Names* by Al Smith.)

HOLLENBACK CIRCLE (D6)

Hollenbeck Circle was dedicated on May 16, 1966, in Ordinance 188-66. It was named after the property owner, Bill Hollenbeck. Mr. Hollenbeck started a farm in 1952 with a few ponies and in 1959 extended the farm until he finally had 100 head of livestock, including horses. Bill and his son-in-law, George Hajek, set up the Hollenbeck Lake in 1954 on the farm. It is 13 acres and the largest man-made lake in Cuyahoga County. The farm closed in 1970. (It was the same year the Gibbs Farm closed, where the Hollenbecks used to take their cattle. Gibbs farm is now part of the Historical Society's and City of Parma's property.) The view is perfect, according to Mrs. Margaret Noll, who lives by the lake off Hollenbeck Circle. (See picture 17.) Lakeview Drive runs along the southwest side of the lake. The Lake is also bordered by Fenway Drive on the north side. Information is from former Mayor James Day and George Hajek and Mrs. Margaret Noll.

HOLLY CIRCLE (H5)

Holly Circle was named after the granddaughter of William Hoislbauer I (1902 - 1989). He was the owner and developer of this land. Information was received from Martha Rudy, niece of William Hoislbauer I. This street was dedicated on November 5, 1984, in Ordinance 115-84. Holly's full name is Holly Hoislbauer. Construction in the area was done by the Fragapane Construction Company of 5348 Pearl Road.

HOLLYWOOD DRIVE (D4)

Hollywood Drive was dedicated as a street by the Parma Township on October 22, 1924. Mr. Stahl, who had a major development in Lakeland, Florida, in the 1920's, may have named this street after Hollywood, Florida.

However, Hollywood, California, was much more in the public's eye at the time. This was in 1924 when Hollywood, Florida, was not as well known as it is in the 1990's. H. A. Stahl, the developer, may have wanted to use the name just for the attraction. He never was able to build on Hollywood Drive since he lost everything in the Depression. However, in the 1950's homes on the north side of the street were built and faced the Ridgewood Country Club and Golf Course. They were large brick homes and created an excellent view from the Golf Course. Much later, part of the Golf Course was sold, and homes on the south side of Hollywood Drive were built. (See "H. A. Stahl, A Tribute.") (See picture 2.)

HOPEHAVEN DRIVE (G7)

According to former Mayor James A. Day, this street was named after Bob Hope. Since Cleveland already had a street named Hope, this one was called Hopehaven Drive. The street was dedicated on April 17, 1961, in Ordinance 57-61.

HOUSTON DRIVE (B3)

Houston Drive was dedicated on September 19, 1966, in City Ordinance 349-66. It is part of the Western Heights Estates, and, appropriately enough, this area is located on Parma's far west side, where all the streets are named after western cities, as is this street.

HOWARD STREET (H8)

Howard street was dedicated on June 9, 1955, at the request of Albert Marusa, land owner and developer of this property. There is another dedication date of December 17, 1962, in City Ordinance 164-62. The first is the plat map date and the second is from the records at Parma City Hall. Albert Marusa is the father of Howard Marusa, for whom the street was named. Howard is married to Sandra, and they have two children, Andrew and Wendy. Howard was in the building

business after finishing school. He, however, is now in the insurance business and living in Bay Village, Ohio.

HUFFMAN ROAD (A4)

This road is located on the boundary line between the cities of Parma and Parma Heights. It is located on the former property of A. and M. Hoffman. It appears again that a misspelling has occurred. We have not been able to locate any family whose name was Huffman who might have had this street named after them. At this time it is felt the street was named after A. and M. Hoffman, whose name was on the 1903 County property map. It is interesting to note that Jacob Hoffman owned land in this area in 1892. Amos and Jacob Hoffman owned the same land in 1874. It appears that the Hoffmans might have had a driveway or road on their property as early as 1874. The earliest date of dedication was found in Parma Heights, which was May 14, 1962.

HUNTINGTON RESERVE DRIVE (E8)

The name "Huntington" was and is a very popular name in the Cleveland area. There was a fort located between Ontario Street and West 9th Street called Fort Huntington where U.S. troops were stationed during the War of 1812. There are the Huntington National Bank, Huntington Play House and Huntington Reserve Park in Bay Village. The developer did not give information that could be verified. Huntington Reserve Drive was dedicated on February 21, 1989, in City Ordinance 47-89.

HOMES BUILT DURING H. A. STAHL'S DEVELOPMENT

Home located on
South Canterbury Road,
built 1929.

14

Home located on
South Canterbury Road,
built 1929.

15

Home located on
South Canterbury Road,
built 1923.

16

17

18

Parma's Lake Hollenbeck. It is a private lake and the largest in Parma. See Lakeview Drive for explanation

Quarry Creek, West Creek, at Ridgewood Drive. See "Quarry Creek: The Forgotten Tributary"

19

20

South Canterbury home built about 1926.

Southington Drive home built in 1931.

21　　　　　　　　　Kerneywood Drive homes, built 1927-1928.

22

This home is located at the corner of Wareham Road and Hampstead Avenue, built in 1920's.

23

This Elsmere Drive home was built in 1926. It is part of the Greenbriar Estates.

24

H. A. Stahl planned many parks and green areas in his development. This is at the corners of Manorford Drive, Kerneywood Road, Keltonshire Road and Ridgewood Lakes Drive.

Somia Drive at South Park Boulevard

26

25

This Onaway Oval home was built in 1926. It is part of the Greenbriar Estates.

27

28

This Elsmere Drive home was built in 1931. It is part of the Geenbriar Estates

This Elsmere Drive home was built in the late 1920's. It is part of the Greenbriar Estates.

29

30

A Ridge Road home near Ridgewood Lake built in the 1920's.

Dartworth Drive homes built in late 1920's.

31

32

A Sheraton Drive home built in 1927.

A Ridge Road home near Ridgewood Country Club built in 1930.

33

Home located on Dresden Avenue.
Built during H. A. Stahl Development in 1929.

34

Home located on Bremen,
built in 1929.

35

Home located on
South Canterbury Road, built in 1927.

36

Salisbury Drive home, built in 1926.

37

Home located on Salisbury Drive,
built in late 1920's.

38

Home located on Salisbury Drive,
built in late 1920's.

39 State Road looking north. Picture taken June 26, 1927. Notice development in the present day Veterans' Memorial Park area (see Dellwood Avenue). Courtesy of the Western Reserve Historical Society Library.

40

The top of the picture shows the homes being built in the 1950's: Norris Avenue, Somia Drive, Priscilla Avenue, Dellwood Drive, Standish Avenue, Alden Avenue, Winthrop Drive, Ridgewood Drive (far to right) and Longwood Avenue (immediately to left). Also shown here, just completed, is Parma Senior High School. *(Property of Parma Area Historical Society.)*

41

Ridgewood Drive and Broadview Road in 1955. Notice open area and lake south of Ridgewood Drive. In the open field north of Ridgewood are where Staunton, Winchester, Yorktown, Williamsburg and Jamestown Drives are located now.

42 Marmore Avenue runs from State Road to West 33rd Street just south of Brookpark Road. Brookview Boulevard is second street south; Woodway Avenue and Freehold Avenue can be seen west of State Road. North Avenue and Tuxedo Avenue are located where the farm is on this picture taken in 1949. Photographer is Robert Runyan, from collection of Bruce Young.

43   This 1949 picture shows Pearl Road, Ridge Road (lower left corner), Brookpark Road and train tracks. Other streets from Brookpark Road are: Velma Avenue, Luelda Avenue, Laverne Avenue and (bottom right) Maysday Avenue. Photographer is Robert Runyan, a Bruce Young Collection.

44 Byers Field in foreground; wooded area top of picture is where the Regency Apartments are now and where Regency Drive, Laurent Drive, Ralston Drive, Williston Drive, Lalemant Drive, Talbot Drive, Lynett Drive and Randolph are also located. Ridge Road is a two-lane road and notice Day Drive missing. Picture taken in 1955.

45 North of John Muir Elementary School; closest to the school is Brookdale Avenue, then Grovewood Avenue and Lincoln Avenue (top of picture). Picture taken in 1950's. Street on left is West 24th Street. Notice the construction on Brookdale Avenue.

46 Notice South Park Boulevard (next to Quarry Creek) at top of picture (See South Park Boulevard for explanation). Other streets are Grantwood Drive, Wales Avenue, Wellington Avenue, Maplecrest Avenue, Parklane Drive and Heresford Drive. Photographer is Robert Runyan, a Bruce Young Collection. Photo taken in 1951.

47 This 1951 photograph shows the intersection of Brookpark and Broadview Roads. Also shown are Brookview Boulevard, North and Tuxedo Avenues (see construction of Brookpark–Broadview Shopping Center); see these streets in this book. Photographer is Robert Runyan, a Bruce Young Collection.

48 The first European settlement (1816) in Parma was by Benajah Fay Family. The settlement was located (in this picture) at what now is the corner of Ridge Road and Theota Avenue. Bradley Avenue is one street north and Wolf Avenue is one street south. All were named after early settlers. One street south of Wolf Avenue is Ridgewood Avenue, which was the beginning of H. A. Stahl's work in Parma. Also shown is Maysday Avenue (lower left) and Kennilworth Avenue (upper right). Picture taken in 1948.

49 Streets from right are Grantwood Drive, Wales Avenue and Wellington Avenue. The school is State Road School. Notice construction on Wales Avenue. Picture taken 1955. Property of Parma Area Historical Society.

50 You will notice behind Pleasant Valley Junior High School the construction on the homes on West 101st Street (Dell Haven Drive), West 99th Street (Mayberry Drive), West 98th Street (Whitaker Drive) and West 96th Street (Chateau Drive). All the above numbered streets were changed to their names on June 26, 1962, in Ordinance 79-62. Reichert Road is also in the picture. Picture taken in late 1950's. Other streets in this development were West 92nd Street (Nobb Hill Drive), West 91st Street (Glenn Oval Drive) and West 94th Street (Hacienda Drive).

51

Brookpark Road and Ridge Road intersection (top right, looking north). Streets from off Ridge Road, south of Brookpark Road, are: Liberty Avenue, Newport Avenue, Manhattan Avenue. (On other side of school) Marlborough Avenue and Kenilworth Avenue. The school is Ridge-Brook Elementary School. Picture taken in early 1950's.

52

Streets in top half of picture are: (from right) Theota Avenue (under construction), Lincoln Avenue, Russell Avenue; parts of Tuxedo Avenue are visible. Picture taken in early 1950's. School is Thoreau Park Elementary School.

53 Parma's Greenbriar Estates were built in the late 1930's. Notice Snow and Pearl Roads and big Creek Parkway. Hauserman Road (bottom right) with Brainard and Windham Drives are shown going off at the bottom of the picture. See Parkland Drive for information on the unique community.

I

INCINERATOR ROAD (A1)

This street is self-explanatory. It was built to serve the city's incinerator and its Ecological Center. It was dedicated on October 6, 1958, in City Ordinance 270-58

INGLESIDE DRIVE (F3)

This is a street developed by Donald Helwick and a partner named Elworthy. Mr. Helwick was a resident of Cleveland Heights and must have known others who lived in the Cleveland Heights–Shaker Heights area who were developing what were known as the Garden Cities. Garden Cities were first developed in England and were special communities set aside from the big cities for what we would call, today, suburban living. These men not only set up communities in this manner but also used the names they found in or around these Garden Communities. The above street is a good example. In England the word *Ingle* means fire, and the name actually means "fireside." There is a town in England called Ingleby, which would seem to mean "by the fire." Ingleside Drive was dedicated on March 23, 1928, at the request of Elworthy and Helwick, the developers. This was part of the Stanford Park Allotment. It might be interesting to note here that H. A. Stahl, who developed the Parma Circle area, used the same name for one of his streets. Did they both get the names from the Garden City Directory or from Shaker Heights, Ohio? The H. A. Stahl street was changed 10 years later to Covington Drive, apparently because of the confusion. (Information is from *Place Names of the English Speaking World* by C. M. Matthews, page 85; local information was secured from Plat Maps at the County Court House.)

IRONWOOD CIRCLE (D8)

This street was dedicated on June 15, 1992, in Ordinance 62-92. It was developed by William DeGraeve and Richard MacKay. It was called the Pine Tree Development. The streets in the Pine Tree Development were all named after golf courses. Ironwood Golf course is located in Hinckley, Ohio, on State Road. The two developers (above) bought this land from the Rini and Allan families. Richard MacKay tells us that a tree on the property called the Moses Oak (after Moses Cleaveland) has been preserved and had a plaque placed on it. It is believed to have been here since before the time of Moses Cleaveland's landing on the banks of the Cuyahoga River in 1796. This street, along with others in the development, is located north of Sprague Road between Ridge Road and York Road. Information came from Richard MacKay, civil engineer and developer.

IVANDALE DRIVE (D4)

This street was dedicated on December 12, 1923. This street is part of the H. A. Stahl Development. It appears H. A. Stahl applied all the ideas in Parma that were used in setting up Shaker Heights; these ideas may be summarized as the Garden City philosophy. Included in this concept were winding roads, lakes, and a golf course. The street names were taken from Shaker Heights streets or taken from the same English sources from which the Shaker Heights streets were named, the Garden Cities of England in the 1920's. H. A. Stahl lived in Shaker Heights in the 1920's and had an office at Cedar and Coventry Roads. Ivandale means "Ivan's Valley." Could Mr. Stahl have named this street after a friend named Ivan? (See "H. A. Stahl, A Tribute.")

Streets and Roads . . . .

I will find a road or make one.

Hannibal

Keep to the common road and thou art safe.

by Petros D. Baz, M.D.
Dictionary of Proverbs

J

JACQUELINE DRIVE (G8)

Jacqueline Drive was dedicated on March 3, 1969, in City Ordinance 64-69. It was named after Jacqueline Demeter, who was one of the daughters of Edward Demeter, who owned the KD Hall on State Road. Mr. Demeter was Director of Purchasing for the City of Parma under Mayor James Day and served on the Planning Commission in the 1960's. He also was in the construction business in the area. Information was received from Gordon Reichwein, a developer.

JAMESON ROAD (D2)

This street was dedicated on December 18, 1919, at the request of the Wooster Park Company (County Plat Books, Volume 67, page 9). Owners of the land were William Wolf, Laura Wolf and James Bingham. President of the Company was W. L. Douglas, and Secretary was H. A. Stahl. Other streets on the same Plat were Ridgefield Avenue, Wooster Parkway, and Arden Avenue. Jameson Avenue has a mixture of older and newer homes and is an attractive residential street. After months of research, there is no definite conclusion as to how this street got its name. Could the Jameson name be taken from James, the first name of Mr. James Bingham, one of the property owners?

JAMESTOWN DRIVE (G4)

This street and a number of other streets in this area were named after early colonial, revolutionary, and patriotic locations. This street is located between Ridgewood Drive and Grantwood Drive off Broadview Road. Jamestown, Virginia, was a town settled by the English London Company in 1607. Jamestown Drive was dedicated December 1, 1964, in Ordinance 271-64. The FTM Company (Fodor-Tilles-Miller) developed this area.

JANICE DRIVE (GB)

Janice Drive was dedicated on October 2, 1967. This street was named after Janice Demeter. She is the daughter of Edward Demeter, who was the owner of the KD Hall on State Road. Mr. Demeter was Director of Purchasing for the City of Parma under Mayor James Day and served on the Planning Commission in the 1960's. He was also in the construction business in Parma for many years. Information is from Gordon Reichwein, a developer, and was verified by the Demeter family. This street was dedicated on October 2, 1967, in Parma City Ordinance 213-67.

JEANNE DRIVE (F6)

According to David Brown, son of Jimmy Brown of Jimmy Brown Realty, this street was named after his mother, Jeanne Brown. This is the same family who owned the Brown Sweet Shop at Snow and Ridge Road from 1932 to 1936. Jeanne Drive was dedicated on March 4, 1957. Information was obtained from Parma City Ordinance 43-57.

JILL DRIVE (G8)

Jill Drive was dedicated on March 3, 1969, in Parma City Ordinance 64-69. This street was named after Jill Demeter. She was a child of Edward Demeter, owner of the KD Hall on State Road. Mr. Demeter was Director of Purchasing for the City of Parma under Mayor James Day and served on the Planning Commission in the 1960's. Mr. Demeter was also in the construction business in Parma for many years. There were four daughters, and all had streets named after them.

JO ANN DRIVE (G8)

This street was named after Jo Ann Demeter. She was the daughter of Edward Demeter, owner of KD Hall on State Road. Mr. Demeter was Director of Purchasing for the City of Parma under Mayor James Day and served on the Planning Commission in the 1960's. Jo Ann Drive was dedicated on March 3, 1969, in Parma City Ordinance 64-69 and County Plat Book 203, pages 47 and 48.

JOHNSON DRIVE (B8)

Johnson Drive was named after the well-known Johnson family. It was dedicated on February 3, 1964, in City Ordinance 26-64. They were early settlers in the Brooklyn/Parma area. The Johnsons owned a large home (a landmark) on the corner of West 25th and Broadview. They owned commercial buildings in the same area. Later they moved to Parma and lived next door to what is now Zabor Funeral Home on Pearl Road. Frank D. Johnson was Mayor of Parma from 1927 to 1934. It is said that John L. Johnson, grandfather of Frank, made money in the California gold rush and returned and built the Johnson house in the Broadview/West 25th Street area (Pearl Road) in 1892. Information is from *The History of Parma* by Ernest R. Kubasek.

JOURDEN AVENUE (F6)

Jourden Avenue had posed a very difficult problem until one day, in connection with research on another matter, the name Jourden appeared in the upper right-hand corner of a plat map where this street is located with N. C. behind the name. According to the County Engineer's office, the people involved here, W. L. Jourden and P. A. Jourden, were developers of the land, but their names were never recorded. This could only be found on the plat map at the Cuyahoga County Library, not at the City Engineer's or County Archives Office. The dedication date was October 15, 1924. Clara and Ed Esper were original owners of the property. Jimmy Brown Realty was involved in developing this community, but his relatives had no information as to the origin of this name. (See Esper Avenue for more information.)

JOYCE DRIVE (A8)

It seems that Joyce Drive was named after the Joyce Construction Company (William Schultz, President, and Edith Schultz, Secretary). This company was doing the construction on the street itself. The street was dedicated on November 7, 1962, in Ordinance 112-62. Joyce

Drive is located on Parma's far southwest corner off Sprague Road. No one was able to testify to this, but it appears very reasonable. All other research turned up no other lead.

JUDY DRIVE (G8)

Judy Drive has a very interesting background. It seems the developer, Gordon Reichwein, anticipated that the Demeter Family would have another girl, so he named this street after the future child, whom they intended to call Judy. There were already four streets named after the four girls in the Demeter Family. As it happened there were no more girls, so the street was really named after no one. Maybe some day we will have an official dedication after someone named Judy. Mr. Demeter was Director of Purchasing for the City of Parma under Mayor James Day and served on the Planning Commission in the 1960's. Judy Drive was dedicated on March 3, 1969, in Ordinance 64-69.

> ## *Did you know that . . . .*
>
> The City of **Lima** was laid out as a town in 1831. Patrick Goode proposed the name, naming it after Lima, Peru . It was incorporated as a town in 1842.
>
> The City of **Lancaster**, Ohio, was laid out by Ebenezer Zane (1748-1812) for whom Zanesville, Ohio, was named. Lancaster, Ohio, was named at first New Lancaster by former residents of the Lancaster, Pennsylvania, area. The New was eventually dropped.
>
> *OHIO PLACE NAMES by Larry L. Miller*
> *University of Indiana Press, 1996*

KADER DRIVE (D8)

This street was named after Joseph Kader Sr., who was Mayor of Parma from 1958 to 1959. He owned the hardware and tire business on State Road. He started his business as a two-pump, one-outdoor-lift gas station in 1937, turned it into a hardware store in 1945, and then took down the gas station in 1951. It was one of the oldest retail businesses in Parma. Joseph Kader Sr. died in 1979. The store is still located on the corner of Grovewood and State Road and is operated as an appliance store by his son Joseph Kader Jr. The Kader family has been very active in this community for many years. Joseph Kader Sr. was very active at St. Francis DeSales Church when it first started in the 1920's. The former Jean Kader, daughter to the former mayor, is the wife to the present Mayor, Gerald Boldt. Another daughter, Ruth, has lived in Parma with her family for many years. Kader Drive was dedicated on October 6, 1958, in Ordinance 200-58.

KELSEY ROAD (E4)

Kelsey Road was dedicated on November 23, 1921. This street is part of the H. A. Stahl Development. It appears H. A. Stahl applied all the ideas in Parma that were used in setting up Shaker Heights; these ideas constitute the Garden City philosophy. Incorporated were the winding roads, lakes, and a golf course. The street names were taken from Shaker Heights streets or taken from the same English sources from which the Shaker Heights streets were named, the Garden Cities of England in the 1920's. H. A. Stahl lived in Shaker Heights in the 1920's and had an office at Cedar and Coventry Roads. (See in this book "H. A. Stahl, A Tribute" for further discussion.)

KELTONSHIRE ROAD (D4)

Keltonshire Road was dedicated on March 17, 1924. It was part of the H. A. Stahl Ridgewood Allotment Number 8. It appears H. A. Stahl applied all the ideas in Parma that were used in setting up Shaker Heights; these ideas constituted the Garden City philosophy.

Included were winding roads, lakes, and a golf course. The street names were taken from Shaker Heights streets or taken from the same English sources from which the Shaker Heights streets were named, the Garden Cities of England in the 1920's. H. A. Stahl lived in Shaker Heights in the 1920's and had an office at Cedar and Coventry Roads. The word "Shire" is equivalent to the American "County" or a similar district of government. It carried with it some sign of prestige. A section of England was named after Sir Kelton, the son of William I, Archduke of Saxons, and it was called Keltonshire. Their battle with Queen Kerala creates interesting reading. From internet http://www.Concentric.net/-Bkelton/Newsaxony.htm. (See in this book "H. A. Stahl, A Tribute" for further information.)

KENILWORTH AVENUE (D2)

Kenilworth Avenue is part of the Tuxedo Heights Allotment. The developer was the Brook Park Realty Company. D. A. Loftus was president. This was one of three streets in this development. The others were Marlborough Avenue and Chesterfield Avenue. It appears that all of these names were taken right from the map of England. There is a town located just south of Birmingham, England, called Kenilworth. Kenilworth Avenue was dedicated on January 26, 1923. Though Theota Avenue was part of this development, it was only the continuation of a street earlier dedicated in 1917. Again, this street was developed at the same time that H. A. Stahl and Don Helwick were developing their Garden City ideas, which were originally begun in England in the early part of the twentieth century. According to C. M. Matthew in her book *Place Names of the English Speaking World*, Kenilworth comes from Kinildewurtha, a twelfth century name; both the lady who owned the farm and the farm itself were known by this name. (See picture 48.)

KENMORE AVENUE (E2)

This street was dedicated on February 7, 1924. This is a street developed by Don Helwick and a partner named Elworthy. Mr. Helwick was a resident of Cleveland Heights and must have known others who lived in the Cleveland Heights–Shaker Heights area who were developing what were known as the Garden Cities. Garden Cities were first developed in England and were special communities set aside from the big cities for what we would call, today, upper-class suburban living. These men (Mr. Helwick included) not only set up communities in this way but also used the names they found in or around these Garden Communities. The above street is good example. There is also a small town in Scotland by the named of Kenmore. It is about 40 miles west of Dundee, Scotland. There is also a street in Shaker Heights (a Garden City) called Kenmore Road. For further information, see in this book, "H. A. Stahl, A Tribute."

KENNETH AVENUE (D2)

Kenneth Avenue was dedicated on April 29, 1920. (Information is from County Plat Maps.) It was part of the Ridgewood Garden Allotments of H. A. Stahl. No one associated with H. A. Stahl (relatives or otherwise) who knew anything about the naming of his streets was found, until we received a letter from an elderly lady, Virginia Brown Fox of Tampa, Florida, on April 25, 1997. She stated that this street was named after Kenneth Payton, the son of George Payton, who was the Sales Manager for the H. A. Stahl Company. Detailed information received from Mrs. Fox leaves little doubt that this street was truly named after Kenneth Payton.

KENTON AVENUE (D4)

Kenton Avenue was dedicated on December 12, 1923. It was part of the H. A. Stahl Ridgewood Subdivision number 3. It appears H. A. Stahl got the name Kenton, as he did for all the streets in Ridgewood Circle (Parma Circle) Development, from the Garden Cities in England. He applied the Garden City philosophy (winding roads, lakes, and a golf course) in setting up his Ridgewood Circle Development. The street names were taken from Shaker Heights streets

or taken from the same English sources from which the Shaker Heights streets were named, the Garden Cities of England in the 1920's. H. A. Stahl lived in Shaker Heights in the 1920's and had an office at Cedar and Coventry Roads. Kenton is a station stop on the London Subway just before the last stop, "Harrow" (see Harrow Drive), on the Central Subway Line. (See in this book, "H. A. Stahl, A Tribute" for further information.)

KERNEYWOOD ROAD (D4)

Kerneywood Road was dedicated on March 26, 1924. It was part of the H. A. Stahl Ridgewood Subdivision no. 9. It appears H. A. Stahl applied all the ideas in Parma that were used in setting up Shaker Heights; these ideas constitute the Garden City philosophy. Incorporated were winding roads, lakes, parks and a golf course. The street names were taken from Shaker Heights streets or taken from the same English sources from which the Shaker Heights streets were named: the "Garden Cities" of England in the 1920's. (Information is from The 75th Anniversary publication on Shaker Heights). H. A. Stahl lived in Shaker Heights in the 1920's and had an office at Cedar and Coventry Roads. In his Lakeland, Florida, development, Kerneywood is the name of one of his streets. Most streets in the Lakeland, Florida, development (called "Cleveland Heights") were names taken from either H. A. Stahl's Ridgewood development in Parma or Shaker Heights. A home on Kerneywood Road was built in 1928 and is a typical example of H. A. Stahl's work in his developments. (See pictures 21 and 24.) Also, see "H. A. Stahl, A Tribute" in this book for further information.)

KEYSTONE ROAD (G3)

Keystone Road was dedicated on November 9, 1925, in Ordinance 133. It took some time to come up with some answers as to the naming of this street. The most plausible answer was discovered after a study of the

Heights developers was made. It was discovered that developer Don Helwick from Cleveland Heights, along with H. A. Stahl of Shaker Heights, had some extensive plans for the Parma area. Could it be that they wanted to make Parma into a Garden City? (See "H. A. Stahl, A Tribute" in this book.) While H. A. Stahl was working on the Parma Circle area, Mr. Helwick was working on the South Park Boulevard Area. It might be noted that South Park Boulevard in Shaker Heights is part of a wealthy community. He called the boulevard running along the west side of the Quarry Creek "Park" by the name South Park Boulevard and the boulevard running along the east side of Quarry Creek Park the name South Park Boulevard East (now Ravine Boulevard). In Parma, South Park Boulevard does not really fit the location as it is on the west side of the would-be park. It is felt that this name was taken directly from Shaker Heights to create prestige. It seems he had intended to use Quarry Creek as a city park, and his plans were to develop beautiful homes on both sides of the park. In his original plans, he had Keystone Road running from Broadview to State Road (now Maplecrest Avenue west of Quarry Creek) with the Quarry Creek Park separating the State Road side from the Broadview side. This was also done for Wellington Avenue. In fact, Wellington Avenue still continues on the Broadview side to West 24th Street, which was then Cross Road. This name, "Keystone" Road, can also be found in Cleveland Heights not too far from where Don Helwick lived. It might be mentioned here also that Quarry Road is found next to Keystone Road in Cleveland Heights. It appears the whole idea of these two developers was to create something like an English Garden City (as the VanSweringen Brothers did in Shaker Heights). The above is a theory, a plausible theory at that. (See "H. A. Stahl, A Tribute," in this book.) Another theory is that the street could have been named after the former owner, A. J. Keyser (1916). However, there is little to support this idea.

KEY WEST DRIVE (G8)

The naming of this street and other streets after Florida cities and places in the Pleasant Valley-Broadview Area was done at the suggestion of James Day, who was Councilman-at-large at the time and soon to be elected Mayor (1962). Key West Drive was dedicated on April 17, 1961, in Ordinance 57-61). It seems that Mr. Day just returned from a vacation in Florida and thought the names would be appealing to the Parma Community. Information is from City Hall cards and former Mayor James Day.

KING RICHARD DRIVE (F6)

King Richard Drive is located in the so-called Robinhood Estates. King Richard Drive was dedicated on April 18, 1966, in Ordinance 151-66. The Robinhood era in history dates from 1300 to 1500, during which time there were two King Richards of England (Richard II, 1377 to 1399, and Richard III, 1483 to 1485), which accounts for the naming of the street "King Richard." This was called the Richard Subdivision #8. Richard MacKay was the developer. With the above history out of the way, it was stated by a fellow employee and by Mr. MacKay himself that Richard MacKay was the "king" that the employees named this street after!

KLUSNER AVENUE (F6)

During the middle 1920's there were many streets laid out in Parma. This is when the great expansion actually started. But many developers lost everything during the Depression, and all building came to a halt. This is what happened to Lazarus E. Klusner, a naturalist, realtor and developer. After laying out what is now called Klusner Avenue, he lost all the land during the Depression. Klusner Avenue is located off State Road, four streets south of Parmadale. Klusner also developed Flowerdale Avenue in Cleveland (just north of Brookpark off Ridge Road). Since he was a naturalist, "Flowerdale" was quite an appropriate name. His son, William B.

Klusner, is now 70 and lives in Solon (1989). Klusner Avenue was dedicated on July 19, 1926, by Parma City Council.

KNOLLWOOD DRIVE (Cl)

No definite information could be found about this street, but it was most probably named after its location, just east of the Big Creek Parkway. This is a residential street for the Knollwood Apartments. It is located just off Brookpark Road near Big Creek Parkway. This is quite an attractive wooded area. The name actually means a "wooded mound." This street was dedicated on June 18, 1953. Two apartment complexes have made this area a very scenic residential area. A divided road, Westview Drive, going into this complex off Big Creek Parkway gives this area a very attractive appearance.

KNOWLES DRIVE (F8)

Knowles Drive was dedicated on January 15, 1962, in Ordinance 3-62. It was named after Allen Knowles, who was president of the South Side Federal Savings Bank. Bonny Builders, who developed this street, named the street after him for all the work he did for them. Mr. William DeGraeve of Bonny Builders gave this information, and Mary Rusch, who worked for Allen Knowles and handled most of the transactions, also verifies this information. At the time this information was given (1996), Allen Knowles was 95 years old, living in Parma. He was described by both DeGraeve and Rusch as "a great man to work for."

KOCH DRIVE (D8)

Koch Drive was dedicated on April 16, 1962, in Ordinance 38-62. It was named in honor of Parma Fire Chief Robert Koch. He was fire chief from 1957 to 1967. He died in office, May 8, 1967, at the age of 53. He lived on Farnsworth Drive. He was a fireman for 28 years and lived in Parma for 42 years. He is a graduate of Parma High School and served

in the Air Force from 1942 to 1945. A resolution (No. 25-67) was made by City Council expressing sympathy to his family on May 15, 1967.

KRUEGER AVENUE (E2)

Krueger Avenue was dedicated on December 1, 1924. The street was named after the owners of the property: Karl (1860 to 1936) and Marie (1864 to 1928) Krueger. The Kruegers owned the land on the northeast corner of West 54th and Snow Road. They owned the double home which still stands at that corner. Karl purchased the land in the late 1800's. He is the one who put in the street and laid out the plat map. Karl was born in Pommen, Germany, on the North Sea and came to the United States in 1881. Karl and Marie had ten children. Louis, our informant, is one of their grandchildren. Paul Krueger, Louis's father, was born in that home at the corner of Snow and West 54th Street. This information was verified from County records, Cuyahoga County Plat Book 89-90, page 21.

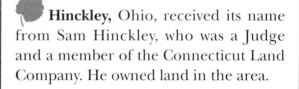

Did you know that . . . .

Hinckley, Ohio, received its name from Sam Hinckley, who was a Judge and a member of the Connecticut Land Company. He owned land in the area.

Canal Fulton, Ohio, was named after Robert Fulton, inventor of the Steamboat. It was named about the time the canal came into existence.

OHIO PLACE NAMES by Larry L. Miller
University of Indiana Press, 1996

LAKEVIEW CIRCLE (C6)

Lakeview Circle (the cul-de-sac area) was at one time Lakeview Drive but was changed to Lakeview Circle on June 3, 1985. It is quite clear that this street takes its name from its location. It runs off Lakeview Drive just west of the Hollenbeck Lake. This is a very attractive residential area. (See Lakeview Drive for more information.) (See picture 17.)

LAKEVIEW DRIVE (C6)

Lakeview Drive runs along the southwest shore of Lake Hollenbeck, and the homes on this street have their backyards on the lake. It is a very attractive area. The lake was formed by the Hollenbeck family years ago when this land was part of their farm. It is the largest man-made lake in Cuyahoga County (13 acres). Part of Lakeview Drive was originally dedicated as part of Arcadia Drive (July 2, 1957, in Ordinance 195-57), but the part of Arcadia Drive from Fenway Drive to what is now Lakeview Circle was changed to Lakeview Drive on June 3, 1985. It was at this time also that part of Lakeview Drive was changed to Lakeview Circle, probably to accommodate the new extension of Lakeview Drive (Ordinance 105-85). The name fits the area exceptionally well. (See picture 17.)

LALEMANT DRIVE (D5)

Lalemant Drive was dedicated on December 5, 1966, in Ordinance 405-66. This developer liked French names and gave many of his streets French names. This word seems to be a corruption of the French word ALLEMENT, which is the word for German.

LANCELOT DRIVE (G7)

Lancelot Drive was dedicated on October 3, 1966. It is located with a group of streets named after English legendary heroes and places. Sir Lancelot was the most famous knight of King Arthur's Knights of the Round Table. However, his excessive love of life led to his downfall along with the knights of the Round Table.

LANGERFORD DRIVE (E6)

Langerford Drive was dedicated on December 28, 1976, in Ordinance 213-76. No one could be found that has this name nor could anyone who worked on this development tell us whom this street was named after. One wonders whether this name comes from two names, Langer and Ford. This type of naming was done by some developers around this time. There is no Langerford in the directory, but there are people by the name of Langer and Ford. The developer said he used the names because of their sound. All areas of research have been tried, but no information given on this matter helped clear up the question. There is a Langerdale Boulevard in South Euclid, but it does not appear to have a connection to Langerford Drive. Other than the above, no definite reason can be given for the naming of this street. If anyone has information on the naming of this street, please call the Parma Area Historical Society.

LANYARD DRIVE (D3)

Lanyard Drive was dedicated on March 3, 1924. This street is part of the H. A. Stahl Development, part of Ridgewood Subdivision number 2. It appears H. A. Stahl applied many of the ideas in Parma that were used in the Garden City philosophy. Included were the winding roads, lakes, playgrounds and a golf course. Apparently the street names were taken from the same English sources from which the Shaker Heights streets were named, the Garden Cities of England in the early 1900's. This is an English word and it comes from the name of a piece of rope or cord worn as a military citation. It is also part of the Middle English "Lanyer," which was a rope holding the whistle hung around the neck. The word first appeared in 1626. H. A. Stahl lived in Shaker Heights in the 1920's and had an office at Cedar and Coventry Roads. (See in this book "H. A. Stahl, A Tribute" for further information.) (Information is from City of Parma, Engineer's Office and information from the Internet.)

LARCH DRIVE (E7)

Larch Drive was dedicated on September 3, 1963, in City Ordinance 183-63. It is part of the Woodbury Hills Subdivision. When we talked with people in the area, they felt this street was named after the larch tree. Two former mayors also said they thought this street was named after the larch tree. Research did not uncover any other reason for naming this street Larch Drive.

LASSITER DRIVE (E6)

Lassiter Drive was dedicated on March 20, 1972, in Ordinance 295-71. According to the developer, this name was given for aesthetic purposes only. No other reason for this name could be found. It might be mentioned that there is a Lassiter Drive in Highland Heights, which is the neighboring village of Lyndhurst (where this developer lived).

LASSITER OVAL (E6)

Lassiter Oval runs west off Lassiter Drive. See Lassiter Drive for information. Lassiter Oval was dedicated on December 17, 1990, in Ordinance 334-90.

LAURENT DRIVE (E5)

Laurent Drive was dedicated on September 5, 1967, in Ordinance number 315-67. The developer said he used French names for his streets simply for aesthetic purposes. Former Mayor Petruska confirmed the developer's remarks. People in history who had this name were Charles Laurent (born in Paris 11-12-1856), first French ambassador (1920-1922) to Germany after World War I; and Raymond Laurent (born in Nimes, France, 7-20-1890), a French political leader. (See picture 44.)

LAVERNE AVENUE (D1)

This street was dedicated on May 12, 1917. The Krather and Koblenzer families owned the land. As it happened, the street was named after one of the Krathers' grandchildren, Laverne Koblenzer Warriner, who was born on March 31, 1904. She was about 13 years old at the time the street was named. Laverne's mother was Susan Krather Koblenzer, and her father was Christian Koblenzer. Information was received from Luelda Krather Barton, a cousin who was interviewed on 12-18-89. A small section of Laverne Avenue (between Pearl Road and Ridge Road) was originally called Pearlridge Avenue and was changed to Laverne on April 6, 1936 (Ordinance 250). (For more information on the Krather family, see Luelda Avenue.) (See picture 43.)

LAWRENCE DRIVE (B8)

Lawrence Drive was dedicated on February 3, 1964 (Ordinance 26-64). There are no homes on this street. Neither residents (corner homes) nor public officials were able to give any reason for the name Lawrence. People who have lived here from the beginning do not know why the name Lawrence was used. West 113th street, the part from Kader Drive to the lot lines on Kader Drive, was changed to Lawrence Drive on March 2, 1964 (Ordinance 48-64).

LEE DRIVE (H6)

This street was named after Robert E. Lee, Southern general during the Civil War. Former Parma Mayor James Day was involved in naming the streets in the Gettysburg Estates of which Lee Drive is part. He had just returned from a trip to the Middle Atlantic States where he visited many Civil War Memorials. He had suggested that they name this development after Civil War personalities and places. Lee Drive was dedicated on December 2, 1968, in Ordinance 396-68. We had just finished commemorating 100 years since the end of the Civil War; this could also have been a catalyst in naming these Civil War streets.

LIBERTY AVENUE (D1)

Liberty Avenue was dedicated on March 31, 1922. This was shortly after World War I and is probably the reason for the naming of this street. This war was fought for the Liberty of all peoples.

It is believed two other streets in Parma were named after generals of World War I also. Liberty was part of the Liberty Heights Allotment by E. Moran. Other streets in the allotment were Manhattan Avenue and Newport Avenue. Can you be more American? (Information is from the Engineer's Office, City of Parma.) (See picture 51.)

LIDO COURT (D6)

Lido Court was dedicated on January 6, 1969, in Ordinance 397-68. According to Julius Paris, the developer, this street was named for aesthetic purposes. In Italy, Lido is the name of a fashionable beach resort near Venice. This resort dates back to 1611 when it was a little lagoon and was referred to as the Latto Maggior; it eventually became Lido. There is also a famous nightclub in Paris called Lido. There is a Lido Beach resort on an island just west of Sarasota, Florida. This sounds like a fashionable name. Information is from the Engineer's Office at Parma City Hall and Parma Regional Library.

LIGGETT DRIVE (F3)

After extensive investigation and after an ad in the *Parma Post* for help in naming this and other streets, Tony Dalesio called the Historical Society and said he always felt, along with other streets in the area (Wood Avenue and Pershing Avenue), that this street and the others were named after World War I generals. General Hunter Liggett (March 21, 1857 to December 30, 1935) was a Lieutenant General in the First World War and Commander of the 1st Corps in Europe in World War I. This street was dedicated on March 3, 1923, only a few years after World War I had ended. This is a real possibility, and unless someone comes up with a better explanation, we will assume it was named after General Liggett.

LIME LANE (D7)

Lime Lane was named after Joseph Lime. Except for three years, Joseph Lime was Auditor of Parma from 1952 to 1976. He worked for Mayors

Zona, Kader, Day, and Petruska. He was not auditor from 1960 to 1963 during the administrations of Mayors Augustine and Bobko. He himself was a candidate for mayor in November, 1959. The street was dedicated in Resolution 61-93 on April 19, 1992. Information is from City Hall records.

LINCOLN AVENUE (E2)

Lincoln Avenue was one of the earliest streets in Parma. The original part of this street was dedicated on December 11, 1907. It was called the F. M. Ranney Allotment. This allotment also included Russell Avenue. Actually, at the time, it was only some forty years removed from the Civil War, so there were many people still living who experienced the Civil War, and President Lincoln was still on their minds. It would seem reasonable to believe that this street was named after President Lincoln. No records could be found to indicate conclusively why this street was named Lincoln. (See pictures 45 and 52.)

LINCOLNSHIRE LANE (G7)

Lincolnshire is the name of the "County" in which the city of Lincoln is located in the east central part of England. It is about 30 miles inland from the North Sea. This is the origin of the name Lincolnshire. This street was dedicated on April 21, 1975, in Parma City Ordinance 25-75, at the request of the Gulfedge Developers.

LINDEN LANES
(North, East, West), (A7, A8)

These streets were all dedicated on December 19, 1957, in Ordinance 352-57. Other streets on the Plat were Millerwood Lane and Martin Drive. The land belonged to H. L. Miller and H. M. Miller and originally was the property of the J. R. Teufel family, who were large property owners in the early days of Parma. One of the Teufel daughters married into the Miller family. A former mayor and a resident said they believe these streets were named after the linden tree. (See Millerwood Lane for further information.)

LIST LANE (A8)

This street was named after the List family. Thomas H. List (1904-1981) owned a 15-acre farm; he and a brother Walter List (1902-1980) developed the farm into a residential area. They built homes in 1958. This street was dedicated on October 6, 1958, in Ordinance 271-58. An extension to List Lane, along with Joyce and Neil Drives in the area, was developed some time later. Our informant was Thomas List's grandson, Thomas List, a principal in the North Royalton School District.

LONGWOOD AVENUE (E4)

Longwood Avenue was dedicated on March 10, 1921. It was part of the Statewood Subdivision. This was a wooded area before the development, and this is probably why it got its name, Longwood. This street was not developed until just before and after World War II. (See picture 40.)

LORIMER ROAD (G3)

Lorimer Road was dedicated on January 15, 1930 (Engineer's Office). Records indicate that this street was laid out and used since 1911. All efforts made to trace the reason for naming this street Lorimer have thus far been fruitless. "Lorimer" is the name of a person who makes bridle bits and spurs. Could this street be named after a man who ran a horse equipment shop in the area some time between 1911 and 1930? History tells us there was a man named James Lorimer, a Scottish jurist who was an authority on international law; he was a professor at Edinburgh in 1862. Anyone having information on the naming of this street is asked to call the Historical Society of Parma, Ohio.

LOURDES DRIVE (G6)

This street was named in memory of the Blessed Virgin's appearance to a girl named Bernadette at Lourdes, France, in 1858. The street was named by the developer, Albert Rispo. The dedication of Lourdes Drive was on October 16, 1989, in Ordinance 324-89.

LOYA PARKWAY (F4)

On May 17, 1993, in Ordinance 97-93, State Road Park Boulevard was renamed Loya Parkway by City Council. It was named in honor of Steve Loya, who through the years has been an important part of Cleveland area softball sports history. In 1990, Steve was entered into the Parma Sports Hall of Fame. Steve died on October 7, 1991, and Parma City Council adopted Resolution 260-91 as a condolence to his family. A note of interest on page 57 is a plat map of a planned development for State Road Park, now Veterans' Park. There are still some signs of this intended development. The entrance to the park across from Ridgewood Drive is what was the beginning of Staten Heights Boulevard. A short section of the street can be seen. The entrance to the State Road Pool on the north side of the fire station was the other end of Staten Heights Boulevard. Both entrances to this road were paved.

LOYOLA DRIVE (E4)

Loyola Drive was dedicated on June 30, 1958, in City Ordinance 169-58. The street was named after Loyola University, a Jesuit institution. The developer was Par Homes; Norman Adler was the president. It was called Ridgewood Subdivision No. 15. It took part of H. A. Stahl's Ridgewood Golf Course, just prior to the City of Parma purchasing it.

LUCERNE AVENUE (F2)

Lucerne Avenue was dedicated on August 26, 1925. It was part of the Lucerne Subdivision by C. C. Wise and H. M. Alexander. There is, of course, a city in Switzerland by this name. Some of the streets in this area were named after World War I generals. Could Lucerne Avenue be named because of some connection with World War I? In England this word also means alfalfa. After many months of research, it is felt that this street was named in connection with World War I.

LUELDA AVENUE (DI)

The 13-year-old young lady for whom this street was named has quite an interesting background. Luelda Gehring Schwab Barton is the granddaughter to Henry Krather, who owned property in the area of Luelda Avenue (Pearl Road/Ridge Road/Brookpark Road area). This street was named after Luelda by her grandfather on May 12, 1917, the date this street was dedicated. Luelda's mother, Permelia Krather, married George B. Gehring and Luelda was born on October 14, 1904. Later in life, Luelda married Lou Schwab. Lou died in 1948 and she later married Jim Barton. An interview with Luelda, age 85, in her Brooklyn home on December 18, 1989, was a real pleasure. The Krather family owned the large brick building on Pearl Road, just before the Brooklyn Bridge in Old Brooklyn. A street in Brooklyn was also named after the Krather family. (See picture 43.)

LYLE AVENUE (F6)

Lyle Avenue is part of the Chestnut Heights Allotment which consisted of Park Drive, Center Drive, Overlook Drive, (Stanfield Drive later on) Esper Avenue, and Jourden Avenue. They were all dedicated on October 6, 1924. This street has been a real stumper. After a number of years of research, nothing has been found to verify the reason for the naming of this street as such. Neither the property owners nor the developers' descendents had any knowledge as to whom or what this street might be named after. Could Lyle be a relative of the Jourden family? (See Jourden Avenue for more information.)

LYNETT DRIVE (D5)

Lynett Drive was named after Mark Lynett, who did much of the work in establishing Parma Community General Hospital. The street is in the vicinity of the hospital. There is also a medical building that bears his name.

Mark was a councilman when he did much of the preliminary work. He was a city official for 15 years, from 1951 to 1966. He held the positions of councilman, clerk of courts and purchasing agent. Mark was also safety director for Mayor Day. Lynett Drive was dedicated on September 15, 1958, in city Ordinance 266-58.

Did you know that . . . .

The city of **Warrensville Heights** was named after the David Warren Family who settled in the area around 1808. The Warrens had eight children. The town was not incorporated until 1957.

The city of **Bedford** was surveyed in 1810 and settled in 1813. It was named after Bedford, Connecticut. One of the earliest settlers was Daniel Benedict.

The city of **Lyndurst** was originally named Euclidville in 1920. It changed its name in 1923 to Lyndhurst. Because of confusion with Euclid, Ohio, the citizens decided to change the name. It was eventually named by a student who submitted the name, Lyndhurst, in a contest.

OHIO PLACE NAMES by Larry L. Miller
University of Indiana Press, 1996

MAGDALA DRIVE (B2)

Magdala Drive was dedicated on June 20, 1955, in city Ordinance 144-55. This was a Forest City Development. This area is located in the northwest part of the city. There is a town named Magdala on the northwest coast of the lake of Gennesaret. It stood on a major route to lower Galilee. This is said to be the home of Mary Magdalene (also spelled Magadala). Though many of the streets in this area have biblical names, most have been named after children or relatives of the developers. It appears that this street was named after the biblical town, as no other explanation could be found. (Information is from *Concordance Dictionary*.)

MALIBU DRIVE (B8)

This street was originally dedicated as West 116th Street by the builder on September 3, 1957, in Ordinance 211-57. However, the residents changed the name to Malibu on September 4, 1962 (Ordinance 104-62). Residents who were able to be contacted could give no reason why they picked the name Malibu. It seems the name might have been chosen because of the popularity of Malibu Beach, California, a wealthy community north of Los Angeles. According to an internet source at the Cuyahoga County Library, the Chevrolet Malibu made its first appearance in 1964 and was discontinued in 1984. The new Chevrolet Malibu car was introduced in 1997. Malibu Drive is located on Parma's far southwest side, just south of Pleasant Valley Road near the beautiful campus of Cuyahoga Community College and Parma's Nike Park.

MALVERN AVENUE
(now West 33rd Street) (F3)

Malvern Avenue was dedicated on March 23, 1923. It was changed to West 33rd Street on May 31, 1932 (Ordinance 57). According to city officials it was done to more easily locate house numbers. This is a street developed by Don Helwick and a partner named Elworthy. Mr. Helwick was a resident of Cleveland Heights and must have known others who lived in the Cleveland Heights-Shaker Heights area who were developing what were known at that time as the Garden Cities. Garden Cities were first developed in England and were special communities set aside from the big cities for what we would today call suburban living. These men not only set up these communities in this way but also used the names they found in or around these English Garden Communities. The above street is a good example of this. Malvern, in old English "Moel Fryn" or "bare hill," is a place in England located near a bare hill, from which it gets its name. There is also a hill in Virginia called Malvern Hill, where one of the important Civil War battles was fought. There is a street in Shaker Heights (a Garden City) called Malvern Road close to where Mr. Helwick lived. (See Sedgewick Road.)

MALVERN DRIVE (C2)

Malvern Drive, which does exist today (see previous entry), is located in an area where all the streets are named after English institutions of learning. No one who knew the developer could say why this street was named as such, but it is felt this street was named after an English town or school since it is located within a group of streets with names of elite educational institutions, some of which are in England (see Roedean Drive). There is a place in England (from the internet) called Malver. This name was also spelled Malverne. Did this street get its name from this English location? There are also streets in Shaker Heights, Rocky River and North Royalton that have this name. Malvern Drive was dedicated on November 6, 1961 (Ordinance 200-61). Malvern Drive is part of a very spacious neighborhood having ranch homes with larger front yards and tree lawns; it is a very attractive area. In English the word "malvern" means a bare hill.

MANASSAS OVAL (H6)

Manassas was another name for the Battle of Bull Run during the Civil War where the north was defeated. This street was named after this battle or battlefield. Manassas Oval is located at the end of Vicksburg Drive in the Gettysburg Estates. It all started back in the 1960's when a member of the city's administration returned from a trip to Gettysburg and the Middle Atlantic States and suggested that streets be named after historic places and battles of the Civil War. Though this street was dedicated some time later, the same theme was used throughout the Gettysburg Estates. This street was dedicated on December 22, 1976, and April 7, 1980, in Ordinance 166-79.

MANCHESTER DRIVE (D4)

Manchester Drive was dedicated on October 22, 1924, as part of the Ridgewood Circle Development. H. A. Stahl was the developer. It appears that he followed some of the ideas the planners of Shaker Heights had in laying out Parma Circle, of which Manchester Drive is a part. Included were the winding roads, lakes, parks, and a golf course. The street names seemed to have been taken from the same English source, the Garden Cities of England in the 1920's. Manchester, England, is located 15 miles west of Liverpool, England, and is about 25 miles from the Irish sea. H. A. Stahl laid out all the streets from just south of Snow Road to Ridgewood Drive and from Westminster Drive to West 54th Street. He had great plans for this "upper class community." However, he lost everything during the Great Depression, and Parma wasn't really developed until the 1950's. (See in this book "H. A. Stahl, A Tribute" for further information.) (See picture 2.)

MANHATTAN AVENUE (DI)

Manahattan Avenue was dedicated on March 31, 1922. It was part of the Liberty Heights Allotment developed by Ettie Moran. Other streets in this development were Newport Avenue and Liberty Avenue. There seems to have been a spirit of freedom, liberty and patriotism, after the First World War, and you couldn't get more patriotic in those days than using the names Manhattan and Newport.

According to Henry Moscow in his book on New York streets, "Manhattan" is an Indian word that loosely translated means "a place where we all got drunk." (See picture 51.)

MANORFORD DRIVE (D4)

Manorford Drive was dedicated on March 26, 1924. This street is part of the H. A. Stahl Development. It was part of Ridgewood Allotment #9. It appears H. A. Stahl applied many of the ideas in Parma that were used in the Garden City philosophy (Shaker Heights, Cleveland Heights). They used the winding roads, lakes, and a golf course. The street names were taken from Shaker Heights streets or taken from the same English source from which the Shaker Heights streets were named, the Garden Cities of England in the 1920's. H. A. Stahl lived in Shaker Heights in the 1920's and had an office at Cedar and Coventry Roads and was well aware of the developments in Shaker Heights and Cleveland Heights. There are actually two names here, *Manor* and *Ford*. Could it have been the Ford's Manor, or a dwelling by the water? (See in this book, "H. A. Stahl, A Tribute" for further information.)

MAPLE DRIVE (G7)

Maple Drive was dedicated on October 22, 1956, in Ordinance 246-56, at the request of Frank Musso, developer. The maple tree was very popular in Parma and was used by the city on various streets on the tree lawn plan. Maple Drive had the Irish Norway maple planted on its tree lawns in the 1960's. This was clearly an aesthetically named street. It is a street of handsome brick ranch homes. Maple Drive runs into Thorncliff Boulevard, which runs along Quarry Creek's ridge and is a very attractive neighborhood. (Information is from Ernest R. Kubasek's book *The History of Parma*.)

MAPLECREST AVENUE (E3)

Maplecrest Avenue was dedicated as Maplecrest on November 9, 1925. However, the part east of

State Road was not its original name. It was changed to Maplecrest Avenue from Keystone Road. It apparently was named originally Keystone Road as part of the continuance of Keystone Road from the east side of the Quarry Creek (Park)–Broadview Road area. (See Keystone Road for further information.)

MAPLEWOOD ROAD (A7)

The major part of this street is in Parma Heights. The part in Parma was dedicated on October 15, 1956, in Ordinance 231-56. It is a tree-lined street, a mile long, and has a very attractive appearance. This is an aesthetic name and it seems to fit the street quite well. The developer was Basilio Imbrigiotta.

MARDA DRIVE (F6)

Marda Drive presents a problem to researchers. The name itself really arouses one's interest as you can imagine it to be the name of a small child, possibly the daughter of a land owner or someone involved in the laying out of the street. Marda Drive was dedicated on September 6, 1960 (Ordinance 169-60). Every angle possible was considered. All involved in the developing of this street or their next of kin were contacted. No one could identify Marda. This street runs from Lyle Avenue to Parkview Drive. We would appreciate if anyone knowing anything about this name could contact the Historical Society.

MARIETTA AVENUE (G2)

Marietta Avenue was set up by E. Moran in his Tuxedo Farms Allotment. It was dedicated on April 28, 1922. Mr. Moran's relatives have not been located. This street is part of a very interesting history of Northeast Parma and Brooklyn Heights. Some of the streets in this allotment were set up in Brooklyn Heights and the names were carried right on into Parma. Tuxedo Avenue is a good example. It is not certain why Mr. Moran picked the name Marietta, unless there might have been some connection to Marietta, Ohio, which has an early history.

MARIONCLIFF DRIVE (F3)

This street was actually named after Clifton Snow and his daughter Marion. Clifton Snow and Ann (Thompson) Snow, his wife, were major property owners in Parma in the early 1900's. Snow Road was named after them. It was some years after his wife's death that this street was named. Other streets in the community were also named by the Snows. The Snows were descendents of the Pilgrims at Plymouth Rock. A genealogy is on file at the Parma Area Historical Library. This street was dedicated on February 2, 1928.

MARKO LANE (F7)

Marko Lane was part of the Gulfedge Developers' plan for the so-called "Robinhood Estates." It runs off Meadow Lane to Dentzler Road. Eleanor Boehnlein reported that she used to live on Marko Lane and that her maiden name was Marko. She said her brother used to play in the woods in this area before Marko Lane was put in. She said her brother carved their name on a large rock close to where the road is now. She doesn't know for sure, but speculates that the developers might have spotted the name on the rock and given the street this name. With extensive research (a check of classical literature through teachers of literature and public libraries did not turn up any character, minor or major, in the Robinhood tales by this name) yielding no other lead, and this being so out of context of names used in the Robinhood Estates, this explanation doesn't seem out of the question. It seems that this Marko family may, in some way, have had an effect in naming this street. Marko Lane was dedicated on May 11, 1959, in City Ordinance 88-59. If anyone has information on the naming of Marko Lane, please contact the Parma Historical Society.

MARLBOROUGH AVENUE (D2)

Marlborough Avenue was dedicated on March 15, 1926. It was part of the Tuxedo Heights Allotment by Brookpark Realty. An extension of the street was dedicated in 1961. Again, this street was named after English place names as most of the developers in Parma opted to do in the 1920's. Marlborough is a little town between London and Bristol (on the Bristol Channel). Many called these streets the Cigarette Development. Though unusual things like this have been done in the past, it would appear that these were named after English place names since not all the streets have cigarette names, but all do have place names. Relatives of the developers could not be found. (See picture 51.)

MARMORE AVENUE (F1)

This street was dedicated on April 28, 1926. It was part of the Brookview Subdivision. Jack Lampl was President and H. J. Marhenke was Assistant Treasurer. After a few years of research, it appears that the street might have been named after H. J. Marhenke, the aforementioned official of the company that developed the street. (Could it possibly be Mar and then "more" letters after? Some builders do strange things in naming streets.) Original owners of the property were Christian and Clara (Seibert) Huy. Their descendents could give no information on the naming of this street. The Huy family was well known in the area. They were married on September 13, 1870, and were well known in the Brooklyn-Parma area. They owned the Shadyside Diary. They had a child, Elsie, who married another developer in Parma, Oswald Kobelt. Besides the Huy family, the Lampl and Wanner families of the developers were also contacted, but they could give no information. (See picture 42.)

MARTIN DRIVE (A7)

This street has a very interesting history. It was dedicated on December 19, 1957, in City Ordinance 352-57. It appears it was named after Martin Teufel, who owned this land at the turn of the century. There is strong evidence to indicate this; however, it could not be verified. Martin Teufel was the great grandfather of the present Teufels (who were contacted concerning this matter) and his family had a

farm on this land. The Teufel name seems to have disappeared from the scene in Parma, and the name Miller seems to have taken its place when Helen Teufel married into the Miller family. The development of this street, Millerwood Lane, and Linden Lanes (North, South East and West) were developed by the H. L. Miller Family. (See Millerwood Lane for more information.)

MAYBERRY DRIVE (C7)

Mayberry Drive was given its name by the people on the street on June 26, 1962 (Ordinance 79-62). They voted on this name after they got permission from the city to change the name from West 99th Street. Eleanor Schredl, who lives on this street, is the one who suggested this name. She suggested this name because of the Andy Griffith TV program that was popular at that time. The whole community voted on the change. (See picture 50.)

MAYSDAY AVENUE (D2)

Maysday Avenue was dedicated on October 10, 1919. No one contacted could give a reason for the naming of this street. Of course there is *Mayday*, which comes from the French word *M'aidez*. This seems very unlikely. This is a very short street that runs between Ridge Road and Pearl Road just north of the Ridge-Pearl intersection. If anyone has information on this street, please contact the Parma Historical Society. (See pictures 43 and 48.)

MAZEPA TRAIL (G5)

Mazepa Trail is part of the Southern Hills Estates. It was dedicated on December 19, 1988, (Ordinance 361-88). This street was named after Ivan Stepanovich Mazepa (1644-1709), a leader of the Ukranian people. He is said to have built many churches for the Ukranian people. He was considered an educator and built institutions of learning for them. He was a Cossack leader who fought to unite the Ukraine into an independent state. He fought against the Russians and he died in exile in Moravia after he was defeated by Peter the Great of Russia. Information is from the Chopko Construction Company and County Plat Book 244, pages 11 and 46.

MEADOW LANE (F7)

Meadow Lane was dedicated on June 1, 1959 (Ordinance 114-59). It is quite a long and attractive street running from Pleasant Valley Road to Dentzler Road. Streets named Meadow in Cuyahoga County number 18. Streets with Meadow in their name in Cuyahoga County number 51. This name has been used for aesthetic purposes quite often in spite of the fact that in the early days of Cuyahoga County, this land was a forest.

MEADOWLAWN BOULEVARD (G3)

This street was dedicated on February 21, 1927. It is located north of Grantwood Drive, east off Broadview Road. It was developed by R. C. Johnson of the K & L Land Company. It would appear that this is purely an aesthetic name given by the developer. It sounds as if this street has something in common with the other streets in the area. The street directly to the north of it is Parkleigh Drive, which means a "park in the clearing," and to the north of that street is Clearview Avenue. The name of each street indicates a meadow or clearing. Another street in the area is Dartmoor Avenue. Moor, in early English, means a high uncultivated land. Draw your own conclusion. (See Parkleigh for further information.)

MELODY LANE (F7)

Melody Lane was dedicated on December 7, 1959, in City Ordinance 214-59. This was an interesting and attractive name given to this street by Bonny Builders . This is a short street and is located in the southern hills of Parma between Hoertz Road and Pleasantview Drive. Some weather forecasters call this area the secondary snow belt.

MERKLE AVENUE (El)

Emma and Jacob Merkle, farmers from the old Brooklyn area, developed this land into Merkle's Brookpark Subdivision. The street was dedicated on August 31, 1925. And, of course, this street was named after the Merkle Family. Information was received from County Plat Book 91-93, page 24, and from the "Old Brooklyn" Commercial Press, 1979, page 35.

MILFORD AVENUE (F2)

Milford is part of the Torrington Park Allotments. This is a street developed by Don Helwick and a partner named Elworthy. Mr. Helwick was a resident of Cleveland Heights and must have known others who lived in the Cleveland Heights-Shaker Heights area who were developing what were known as the Garden Cities. (Such developers included the Van Sweringens of Shaker Heights and H. A. Stahl of Parma.) Garden Cities were first developed in England and were special communities set aside from the big cities for what we would today call suburban living. These men not only set up areas according to these garden communities but also used the names they found in or around these English Garden Cities. The above street is a good example of this. Milford Avenue was dedicated on August 20, 1924. It appears that the name of this street was either taken from a Garden City Directory or from Milford Road in University Heights near the home of Don Helwick.

MILLERWOOD LANE (A7)

Millerwood Lane was named after the owners of the property, Harold and Helen (Teufel) Miller. The street was dedicated on December 19, 1957, in Ordinance 352-57. It seems that Mr. Miller is the son-in-law to the J. Teufel family, a family who owned whole sections of land in southwest Parma in the 1903 map and in the 1874 map. The Teufel family had a meat business on this farm in the early days. See Martin Drive for further information. Information is from former Mayor James Day and the county Plat Map.

MIRABEAU DRIVE (E6)

This street was dedicated on March 20, 1972 (Ordinance 295-71), as the Sassafras Hills Subdivision. According to the developers, this street was named Mirabeau for aesthetic purposes. There was a French soldier and politician, André Mirabeau. He served in the U.S. Army from 1780 to 1785 and then returned to France during the French Revolution. He lived from 1754 to 1792. Other notable French men by that name were Gabriel Honore Mirabeau (1749 to 1791) and Victor E'Riquette Mirabeau (1715 to 1789). This name is also a title given to the count of Mirabeau.

MONMOUTH DRIVE (D4)

This street, located off Parma Circle, appears to have been named after a town at the mouth of the River Monnow called Monmouth, England, which is on the Wales/English border about five miles north of the Severn River. It was a center of Catholic activity in the 1670's. The area around Monmouth must be quite nice inasmuch as King Arthur's legendary Camelot was supposed to be located somewhere in this area. This is an H. A. Stahl Development; see page 21. (See *Place Names of the English Speaking World* by C. M. Matthews, page 97.)

MONTAUK AVENUE (E2)

Montauk Avenue was dedicated on August 20, 1924, by Elworthy and Helwick in the Torrington Park Allotment. The Iroquois Realty was also involved. Research indicates that there was a Montauk Indian tribe from New York State. Did the Iroquois Realty have something to do with the naming of this street? This sounds like a good possibility, but we could not find anyone to verify this conjecture.

MOONCREST DRIVE (E6)

Mooncrest was dedicated on December 17, 1979, in Ordinance 190-79, at the request of Sunrise Builders. This street is located among a group of streets given very descriptive astronomical names. Other streets such as Night Vista Drive and Eventide Drive are in this quite attractive development.

MOORE DRIVE (C6)

Moore Drive was named after Charles Moore, who was a Safety Director during Mayor Joe Kader's administration (1958-1959). He was on the Planning Commission during Parma's rapid growth in the 1950's. He was also manager for Mayor Joseph Kader's election campaign. He lived on Brookview Boulevard in Parma. Moore Drive was dedicated on May 20, 1957, in Ordinance 107-57.

MORNINGSIDE DRIVE (E3)

Morningside Realty and developers seem to be responsible for the naming of this street in the Morningside subdivision. This street runs off West 54th Street into Dartworth Drive. This seems to have been a street laid out by H. A. Stahl but never dedicated by him. He lost everything in 1930 during the Depression. The street was dedicated on March 24, 1931.

MUNICH DRIVE (C8)

This street was named as such because it is in the proximity of German Central Farm. The street was dedicated on March 2, 1970, in Richard Subdivision #9 in City Ordinance 396-69. Munich is a city in southern Germany. Other streets in the area are Ruhr Drive, Vienna Drive and Baron Drive. Information is from Gordon Reichwein, developer.

NAOMI DRIVE (B2)

Naomi Drive was dedicated on June 20, 1955, in Ordinance 144-55. This street and other streets in this area were given biblical names but were generally named after the children of the developers. This street, however, may have been named after the biblical character, as no one could be found who could identify the person this street was named after. Naomi, a widow, is a biblical character who got Ruth to marry Boaz, one of Naomi's relatives. From this marriage was born Obed, King David's grandfather. Naomi was the wife of Elimelech and mother-in-law to Ruth. She was a leader and counselor in her family.

NASSAU DRIVE (B8)

Nassau Drive was originally dedicated as West 119th Street and was changed to Nassau Drive on September 4, 1962, in Ordinance 104-62. It was originally called West 119th street and dedicated as such October 21, 1960 (Ordinance 216-60). Nassau is a city on one of the Bahama Islands (New Providence Island) off the coast of Florida. It is the capital city of the Bahama Islands. One neighbor said that he liked this name because it reminds them of a warm climate. Another neighbor said that they wanted Dawn Haven, but some other street took that name, so they took their second choice, which was Nassau. In 1962 there were numerous streets that had their names changed from number streets to named streets. Nassau Drive was one of them. Actually the name Nassau dates back to the time of Charlemagne. A street in New York with the name Nassau Street was named after a principality in Germany that belonged to the Royal Family in the Netherlands in the 1600's. Information is from the *Street Book of New York City* by Henry Moscow.

NATHAN DRIVE (B2)

Nathan Drive was dedicated on June 20, 1955 (Ordinance 144-55). Nathan, a biblical character, was King David's chosen advisor. He was a man of God and did not care what man

thought, but spoke God's truth. He was a "fearless upright man" as he was described by William P. Barker, editor of *Everyone in the Bible*, published by Fleming H. Revell Co. in Westwood, New Jersey (1966).

NEIL DRIVE (A8)

Neil Drive was dedicated on October 7, 1968, in Ordinance 257-68. This street and its extensions of List Lane and Joyce Drive were dedicated on this date. The former owner and builder on this property, Henry Bruscino, had a brother-in-law named Neil Sabino who was involved in the construction as a carpenter. Mr. Bruscino didn't feel the street was named after him but didn't know for sure. Neil is not living at this time. Could this street have been named after him? No one seems to know for sure. No one in the construction company, or the engineering company, knew whom the street was named after. The construction of Joyce Drive was done by the Joyce Construction Company, which is not in business at this time. Might the naming of Neil Drive have something to do with the Joyce Construction Company? However, we could get no information to verify this. We have no other leads after many hours of research. If anyone has information concerning the naming of this street, or can verify the above information, please contact the Parma Historical Society.

NELSON BOULEVARD (G8)

Nelson Boulevard was developed by Nelson Homes, Inc. The president of this company was Hugh Nelson Sr. The development was called the Parmawoods Estate. The family name is given to this street. The dedication of Nelson Boulevard was on May 7, 1973, in Ordinance 33-73. There was also a dedication date of July 8, 1970. (See Brian Drive for more information on Hugh Nelson Sr.)

NELSON DRIVE (G8)

Nelson Drive was dedicated on December 1, 1964, in the Pleasant Acres Estates #1. See

Nelson Blvd. and Brian Drive for further information on this street. There was also a dedication date of October 2, 1967, in Ordinance 213-67.

NEWCOMB DRIVE (D6)

This street was dedicated on October 7, 1974, in Ordinance 39-74. Paris Development Corporation was involved. The street was named after Fred Newcomb, a long-time Service Director and Planning Commission member during the 1950's. Fred Newcomb lived on Hauserman Road. Newcomb Drive was named after him, posthumously, for his dedicated service.

NEWPORT AVENUE (DI)

Newport Avenue was dedicated on March 31, 1922. It was part of the Liberty Heights Allotment by E. Moran. Other streets in this development were Manhattan Avenue and Liberty Avenue. This Allotment was developed shortly after the First World War. Can you get more patriotic? This street was probably named after Newport, Rhode Island. We have no personal witness to testify to this, though. (See picture 51.)

NIGHT VISTA (D6)

Night Vista Drive was dedicated on July 16, 1979, in Ordinance 105-79. This street is located in a group of streets given very descriptive astronomical names. Other streets such as Mooncrest Drive and Eventide Drive are in this quite descriptive group. Sunrise Builders were the developers.

NOBB HILL DRIVE (C7)

Nobb Hill Drive was originally dedicated as West 92nd Street on June 17, 1957 (Ordinance 156-57). The name was changed to Nobb Hill by the residents on June 26, 1962 (Ordinance 79-62). Mrs. Thomas Chipoaro, a resident of Nobb Hill Drive, said they got the name, she believes, from the Nobb Hill in San Francisco. Eleanor

Sadowski remarked that their street climbs slightly from one end to the other, which is one of the highest points in the area. She feels that this is how the street got its name. (See picture 50.)

NORFOLK DRIVE (G3)

Norfolk Drive was dedicated on December 1, 1964 (Ordinance 271-64). It is located in a group of streets named after patriotic places. The city of Norfolk was founded in 1682. It was burned by the patriots to prevent capture by the British during the Revolutionary War. It is located near the world's largest naval base. The town was rebuilt in 1805 and became a city in 1845. Its present population is 261,250.

NORMANDY DRIVE (F6)

Normandy Drive was dedicated on July 15, 1963, in Ordinance 164-63. It was part of what is called the Normandy Subdivision. Normandy is where allied troops landed on D Day for the invasion of Europe (June 6, 1944). Though this was almost 20 years after the invasion, it was still on people's minds. Normandy High School was opened in 1968.

NORRIS AVENUE (F4)

This street was named by the Trustees of the Estate of Mary Norris, Philip David Norris and Harry Farnsworth. The Norris family owned the property where this street was laid out. Norris Avenue was dedicated on June 8, 1925. (Information is from County Plat Book 91-92, page 18, and a 1903 Parma Property ownership map.) (See picture 40.)

NORTH AVENUE (Fl)

This street is tied in with Tuxedo Avenue, and it appears that it got its name from Brooklyn Heights, Ohio. E. Moran, the developer of the Tuxedo Farms Allotment, divided the land from New Brooklyn Heights Town Hall to the Brooklyn city line into three main streets. The one north of Tuxedo Avenue was called North

Street, and the one south was called South Street. Later Tuxedo Avenue and North (Street) Avenue were developed further into Parma. South Street was never extended into Parma. In Parma, the street was dedicated on April 27, 1925. (See pictures 42 and 47.)

NORTH CANTERBURY ROAD (D4)

North Canterbury Road runs from Ridgewood Circle northeast to Allanwood Road. Canterbury is the name of a cathedral town in England just southeast of London. This street was dedicated on June 28, 1922, at the request of H. A. Stahl. North Canterbury Road was part of Stahl's plans for a Garden City. This street is part of the winding roads, parks, lakes and golf course that were so characteristic of a Garden City. (For further information see "The Garden City" and "H. A. Stahl, A Tribute," in this book. (See picture 2.)

NORTH LINDEN LANE (7A)

See "Linden Lane."

NORTH MIAMI DRIVE (F8)

This street, part of the State-Sprague Subdivision by Slabe-MacKay, was named after a suburb of Miami, Florida. It is interesting to note that there is no Miami Drive, but there are a North Miami and East Miami. In this subdivision, most streets were named after Florida cities. North Miami Drive was dedicated on January 17, 1977, in Ordinance 214-76. This was the second of two groups of streets named after Florida cities.

NORTH SARASOTA DRIVE (F7)

North Sarasota Drive was originally dedicated on November 16, 1964, through City Ordinance number 245-64 as West 38th Street. It was changed to North Sarasota Lane on November 8, 1967, in Ordinance 398-67. According to resident Albert J. Martin, the name "North" Sarasota was chosen in relation to the Sarasota Drive in their community, not

after a possible suburb of Sarasota City in Florida (compare North Miami). For further information on Florida streets, see Winterpark Drive.

NOTTINGHAM DRIVE (F6)

This is the name of a location in north central England, a place that is referred to in the Robinhood tales. This street is located in a group of streets that have been named after characters and locations in the Robinhood Tales. It was dedicated on July 5, 1960, in Ordinance 129-60.

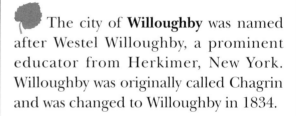

Did you know that . . . .

The city of **Willoughby** was named after Westel Willoughby, a prominent educator from Herkimer, New York. Willoughby was originally called Chagrin and was changed to Willoughby in 1834.

The city of **Wadsworth,** Ohio, was named after General Elijah Wadsworth, a Revolutionary War veteran from Connecticut. He owned the majority of the property in the area which he purchased in 1799. Wadsworth became a city in 1911.

The town of **Novelty,** Ohio, took its name from what they called a Novelty stop on a Railroad line which stopped to pick up passengers and milk at this location. This information originally came from the Russell Women's Civic Club.

OHIO PLACE NAMES by Larry L. Miller
University of Indiana Press, 1996

O

OAKDALE ROAD (C2)

Oakdale Road was dedicated on August 28, 1919. It is part of the Tuxedo Lake Park Allotment. This name was given for aesthetic purposes. Oak trees are in the area, and Oakdale is a good name to describe this area between the Metroparks and what is now called Evergreen Lake.

OAKLAWN DRIVE (G3)

Oaklawn Drive was dedicated on July 19, 1965; another dedication date is July 5, 1966, in Ordinance 213-66. It is part of the Richard Subdivision number one. This street is located near the Quarry Creek area, near Midtown shopping center. The streets in Subdivision one were all developed out of a wooded area. The woods and park-like setting can still be seen at Quarry Creek Valley, a short distance from Oaklawn Drive.

OAKWOOD ROAD (A7)

Oakwood Road was part of the Basilio Imbrigiotta Allotment number 3. John Pentz was also builder and developer. It was dedicated (in Parma) on June 2, 1958, in Ordinance Number 144-58. This appears to be an aesthetically named street. This is a long street extending into Parma Heights, part of an exceptionally neat residential area.

OAKWOOD OVAL (D8)

Oakwood Oval is part of the Pine Tree Development. All the streets in this development were named after golf courses. Oakwood Golf Course is located in Cleveland Heights, Ohio. Oakwood Oval was dedicated on April 19, 1993. This is a Richard MacKay Development.

OCALA DRIVE (E8)

Ocala Drive is part of State-Sprague Subdivision laid out by Slabe/MacKay in the 1970's. Ocala was dedicated on January 17, 1977, in Ordinance 217-76 and is part of what might be called the second Florida Estates.

Ocala is the name of a city in north central Florida near the Ocala National Forest. See Orlando Drive, below, or Winterpark Drive, below, for further information.

OLD PLEASANT VALLEY ROAD (A6)

On April 19, 1954 (Ordinance 63-54), Council ordered the "extension" of Pleasant Valley Road to West 130th to meet Bagley Road. But they called it East Bagley Road. At this point in time, Pleasant Valley Road, from Oakwood Road to Pearl Road, became known as Old Pleasant Valley Road. No ordinance could be found for the changing of the name to Old Pleasant Valley Road. See Pleasant Valley Road for further information.

OLD ROCKSIDE ROAD (H2)

Old Rockside Road was actually Rockside Road until the mid 1950's when Snow Road was extended to Broadview from State, and Rockside was extended from where Pinnacle Park Drive is now directly east to Snow Road. Now the Old Rockside Road terminates before it enters Seven Hills and appears to never have been part of Rockside Road. It is an excellent picture of what Historic Rockside Road was from Broadview Road to Brecksville Road before the 1950's. Old Rockside Road also has the privilege of having the oldest home in Parma, which is also a one-family-owned home at that, and one of the greatest historic landmarks in the area: the Henninger house at the corner of Old Rockside Road and Broadview Road. (See Rockside Road for further information.)

ONAWAY OVAL (C2)

Onaway Oval was dedicated on December 12, 1939. It is part of the Greenbriar Estates, an exclusive community in the 1940's, 1950's, and 1960's. All the street names in this community were taken from street names in Shaker Heights, including this street. This was an exclusive upper class community. One had to be approved by a board before moving into Greenbriar. The rules of approval went by the wayside in the 1970's. This appears to be a continuation of H. A. Stahl's plan for a Garden Community. For further information see Parkland Drive and also "H. A. Stahl, A Tribute." (See picture 53.)

ORCHARD AVENUE (D2)

Orchard Avenue was a street developed just prior to the Garden Cities development of H. A. Stahl. This was the Wooster Park Land Company. As it happened, H. A. Stahl was Secretary of this Company, and it appears that is how he got his start in Parma. The street was dedicated on September 13, 1919. Orchard Avenue was probably named after an orchard in the area. This could not be verified, however. This has been the case with other streets with such names. Research on the following families revealed nothing. The owners of the property were George and Minnie Friedrich, and Ira D. and Barbara Siegfried. Other owners in the area were Emma Ball and W. L. Douglas.

ORCHARD PARK DRIVE (E5)

Orchard Park Drive was originally called Forest Drive (dedicated on September 22, 1922). It was changed to Orchard Park Drive on May 16, 1932 (Ordinance Number 55), because there was another street in Parma with the same name. Orchard Park Drive was an appropriate name since it was developed in the middle of an orchard. Fruitland Drive, next to it, was also named after this orchard. Information about the orchard was given by Jim Corson, who has lived on Fruitland for many years. The large orchard can be seen in the 1949 aerial photos.

ORCHARDVIEW ROAD (H8)

Orchardview Road received its name from its location. According to Marvin Zelman, an early area resident, there was a large orchard in this area that could be seen from Broadview Road and extended to Robert and Howard Streets. Orchardview Road was dedicated on December 17, 1962, in City Ordinance 164-62.

ORLANDO DRIVE (G8)

Orlando Drive was dedicated on April 17, 1961. It is part of the so-called "Florida Estates." It seems that after Councilman-at-large James Day, and soon to be Mayor, returned from a trip to Florida, he suggested that these streets be named after Florida cities. Information is from Ordinance 57-61 and from former Mayor Day.

OVERLOOK ROAD (C2)

Overlook Road is part of the Tuxedo Lake allotments. It is a short street connecting Westmoreland Drive to Evergreen Drive. This whole complex was dedicated on August 30, 1919. Frank Johnson was the developer. This street completes the circle around Evergreen Lake. This is a very attractive and natural setting for a residential area. There are 18 streets in Cuyahoga County with this name. According to city records, part of Stanfield Drive in Parma was also called Overlook Drive at one time. It was changed in 1932. Brookdale Avenue, part of the Tuxedo Farms allotments, was also called Overlook Avenue but its name was changed on November 9, 1925. It is also possible that Twin Lakes Drive was called Overlook Drive at one time. However, in some documents, this street was called Overland Drive. It seems this name was quite appealing to the northeast Ohio communities.

OXFORD DRIVE (D4)

Oxford Drive was dedicated as a street on March 26, 1924, at the request of H. A. Stahl. He named most of the streets he laid out after English cities. Oxford is no exception. Besides being a university, Oxford is also a town about 25 miles east–northeast of London. For further discussion see "H. A. Stahl, A Tribute."

P

PANAMA DRIVE (F8)

Panama Drive was dedicated on October 8, 1987, in Ordinance 183-87. It is one of the later streets developed in the State Road/Sprague Road Florida Estates. This street was named after Panama City in the Florida Panhandle. For further information on this street see Winterpark Drive.

PARK DRIVE (F5)

Park Drive was dedicated as part of the Chestnut Heights Allotment on October 6, 1924. Park Drive runs from State Road to "Quarry Creek Park." It appears that this was part of a large scale park plan for Quarry Creek from which this street got its name. Though Parkview Drive, which is the continuation of Park Drive (or South Park Boulevard?) was not developed until 1927, it appears that this park plan was intended on the original plans from the earliest developers. The full Park of Quarry Creek did not really develop, but only small areas have been preserved as a park. Again, the Depression seems to have been responsible for another setback for the Village of Parma. The City of Parma still owns Quarry Creek land in the area from Broadview Road to Snow Road, which, it appears, was supposed to be part of this park.

PARKHAVEN DRIVE (G6)

Parkhaven Drive was dedicated on October 6, 1958 (Ordinance 281-58). It was named by the developer, John Pentz. Parkhaven Drive runs off Broadview to East Parkview Drive, which runs along Quarry Creek. Part of this area is a city park. See Park Drive for further information. Many streets in this area have "park" in their name probably because of the attractiveness of the Quarry Creek as a park.

PARKLAND DRIVE (C2)

Parkland Drive was dedicated on December 4, 1939, in Ordinance 53-39. It is part of the Greenbriar Community of Parma that was set up with the idea of an exclusive community in mind. For about 15 to 20 years, there were rules governing Greenbriar Estate, and residents had to be approved before moving into the community. It was dedicated sometime after H. A. Stahl developed Parma Circle, but his ideas known as the Garden City Philosophy seem to have been prevalent throughout the development of this property. However, many of the homes were built during the time of H. A. Stahl's work on Ridgewood Circle, years before the street was dedicated. All the streets in the Greenbriar Estates were named after streets in Shaker Heights, the ideal Garden City. There were large homes on this street where upper to upper middle class people would live. This exclusive philosophy was dropped in 1973. People involved in the development of Greenbriar Estates were: Sarah Hauserman, probably a property owner, Frank D. Johnson, an attorney, A. F. Humel and G. J. Greiner. The Bank was the Pearl Street Savings and Trust Bank. See "The Garden City," page 18.

PARKLANE DRIVE (F3)

Parklane Drive was dedicated on July 12, 1923. This street runs from State Road to South Park Boulevard (Quarry Creek) and is what Mr. Don Helwick would probably have called Quarry Creek Park. Mr. Helwick, the developer, was a resident of Cleveland Heights and must have been well aware of the Garden Cities developments, since Cleveland Heights and Shaker Heights were described as Garden Cities. Garden Cities were first developed in England and were special communities set aside from the big cities for what we would today call wealthy suburban living. He and others not only set up communities on this order but also used the names they found in or around these Garden City communities. The above street is a good example. However, before Mr. Helwick could complete his work, the Depression hit and hit him hard. He lost everything during the Depression. Later this street, as well as other streets in the area, was developed into middle class housing for returning veterans in the late 1940's and 1950's. (For more information see "Don Helwick, A Man with a Plan" in this book.) (See picture 39.)

PARKLEIGH DRIVE (G3)

Parkleigh Drive was dedicated on March 21, 1927. The developers were K. and L. Land company (Klein-Lampl). R. C. Johnson was also an officer in the company. Leigh comes from the English "leigh" (lea, ley), which in later English meant a clearing. Many village names added "leigh" onto their names because they built their towns in clearings. This is analogous to a calling Mt. St. Mary's School as such because it was built on a mountain. It is interesting because the street to the north is called Clearview Avenue and to the south Meadowlawn Boulevard. Relatives of Mr. Lampl could give no information for the naming of these streets. Information is from *Place Names of the English Speaking World* by C. M. Matthews, page 57.

PARKSIDE DRIVE (C8)

Parkside is a north-south street that runs between Pleasant Lake Boulevard and Running Brook Drive. It is also located in the vicinity of Pleasant Valley Lake and the German Central Farm. It is a hilly and very attractive area. This and its location near Pleasant Valley Lake Park may explain why this street was called Parkside Drive. Parkside was dedicated on October 9, 1968. Parkside has another dedication date of August 8, 1986, in Ordinance 168-86.

PARKVIEW DRIVE (G5)

Parkview Drive runs along the west side of Quarry Creek. This street was dedicated on May 4, 1927, at the request of the Wilkoff Company. In one city ordinance, part of this street was called West Parkview. This section of the street was dedicated on December 16, 1957. (See Park Drive and Keystone for further information.)

PARKVIEW DRIVE, EAST (G5)

There are actually two sections of this street. One runs along the east side of Quarry Creek Valley, which was dedicated on October 6, 1958, in Ordinance 281-58, and the other runs between Gettysburg Drive and Lourdes Drive, which was dedicated on October 16, 1989, in Ordinance 324-89. Quarry Creek Valley gives this land a park-like atmosphere. Most streets in this area have been given names that have some reference to Quarry Creek Valley.

PARKVIEW DRIVE, WEST (G6)

West Parkview Drive was dedicated on December 16, 1957. It appears this was called "West" to distinguish it from Parkview Drive. Both streets run along the Quarry Creek Valley. Actually, West Parkview Drive is the same street just south of Parkview Drive. The real difference between the two streets is the date of dedication. West Parkview Drive was dedicated on December 16, 1957, and Parkview Drive was dedicated on May 4, 1927.

PARMA PARK BOULEVARD (A7)

Parma Park Boulevard runs between Pearl Road and Pleasant Valley Road. This street presents a problem inasmuch as it was dedicated on April 29, 1925, many years before the present parks in the area were in existence (Nike Park and Nathan Hale Park). J. R. Teufel was the owner of this property at the time, and, according to members of his family, as a hobby, the family had a harness racing track on the grounds of their farm. They maintained this strictly as a hobby and because they loved horses. Could this street have originally received its name from this private park in this area? No one seems to know for sure. (Information is from Parma Plat Map of the Orchard Acres allotment and county Air Photo records.)

PARMAVIEW LANE (F8)

Parmaview Lane is located in the southeastern hills of Parma, and from some of these hills can be seen the northwestern section of Parma and Cleveland, hence the name Parmaview. The street was dedicated on May 11, 1959, by City Council in Ordinance 85-59.

PARMENTER DRIVE (D4)

Parmenter Drive was dedicated on March 26, 1924, in H. A. Stahl's Ridgewood Development #9. It appears that H. A. Stahl applied all the ideas of the Garden City Philosophy to his Parma Developments, the same ideas used in setting up Shaker Heights, Ohio. The winding roads, lakes, and a golf course were all part of this philosophy. The street names were either taken from Shaker Heights street names or from a Garden City Directory from England of the 1920's. This street might be an exception to this rule since it appears that this street might have been named in reference to the city's name (Parma) inasmuch as no such name could be found in our research. However, there were other streets that could not be found; nevertheless, it is felt the names were part of the Garden City planning. (See picture 2.)

PEARL ROAD (D2)

Pearl Road has quite a history. On an 1874 map of Cleveland, Pearl Street was a relatively short street running from Mulberry and Old River Road to Columbus Avenue just south of Lorain Avenue, where it stopped. Columbus Road ran south to old Brooklyn. Later, Columbus Road was changed to Pearl Street, straight through old Brooklyn. Later in 1906, the original Pearl Street was changed to West 25th Street. Pearl Road has been called the Three C Highway (Cleveland, Columbus, Cincinnati Highway), Wooster Pike Road, and I also understand from Kubasek's *History of Parma* that it was called Medina-Wooster Pike and the Brighton and Parma Plank Road. (The first plank road laid in 1867 was Pearl Road; it ran from Cleveland to York Road.) It received its present name, Pearl Road, in Parma, in 1927 (Ordinance 507). It took its name from its Cleveland counterpart which ran into Ohio City. As mentioned above, its name was changed to

West 25th in 1906 from the Brighton (Brooklyn) Bridge north to Cleveland. The Pearl Street Savings Bank (Cleveland Trust) was located on the corner of Clark and West 25th Street (formerly Pearl Road). It became a county road in 1813 and a state road in 1831. Pearl Road became U.S. Route 42 on October 29, 1932. It is believed that it was named Pearl Street as a short side street in Ohio City between 1800 to 1875 possibly being named after some person. Research has not been able to uncover any leads at this time. Interesting note: In New York City, Pearl Street was named for mother-of-pearl, the oyster shell. (See pictures 43 and 48.)

PECAN DRIVE (D7)

Pecan Drive was dedicated on December 7, 1970, in Ordinance 352-70. It was either named after the hard-shelled pecan nut or the pecan tree itself. The name is supposed to be of Algonquin origin. There are other streets in the area named after trees.

PELHAM DRIVE (D4)

Pelham Drive is part of the Ridgewood Subdivision #2 of the H. A. Stahl Properties. It was dedicated on March 26, 1924. There are strong indications that Mr. Stahl picked most of the names of his streets from an English Directory of the Garden Cities of England. Garden Cities in England were for the wealthy people of London, and it is believed the names from these cities were used in the naming of many streets in Parma and Shaker Heights. However, in this case it appears that this may be a name of someone. There is an Englishman of note who has this name, a Henry Francis Pelham (1846 to 1907), who was a professor at Camden University in England. His father, John Thomas Pelham, was a Bishop in England. There is also a New York City suburb by this name, and it is said that the name comes from a man named John Pell, who was given the land where the city of Pelham exists now by the king of England. Mr. Pell named the land after his teacher Pelham Burton. (Yes, it was his first name!) This all happened between 1600 to 1654. There are also a Pelham, New Hampshire, and a Pelham, Georgia. The word itself actually means a "horse's mouth bit with a bar piece." Could the name have come from this actual meaning of the word? It is interesting to note that "ham" in Early English means "place of residents;" could this mean Pell's home? We may never know for sure; take your pick. For more information see "H. A. Stahl, A Tribute."

PERSHING AVENUE (E2)

A phone call from Tony Dalesio confirmed our belief that this street was named after General John J. Pershing, a famous general in the First World War. He mentioned that this street and two other streets (Wood Avenue and Liggett Avenue) were also named after generals of the First World War. All other avenues of research have brought no clearer explanation. The date of dedication, which would also support this assumption, was May 1, 1920. General Pershing lived from September 9, 1860, to July 15, 1948. He was made general by an Act of Congress. He was the first general to hold the honor of Commander of US Forces in Europe. He was born of humble parents in Missouri and taught school before winning admittance to West Point. He fought the Spanish in Cuba in 1898, and the Moros of Mindanao in the Philipines in 1903, at which time he became a Brigadier General. He commanded the 1916 expedition into Mexico. In 1917, he was chosen to head the U.S. Troops in Europe in the First World War.

PIN OAK DRIVE (D7)

Pin Oak is part of the Dogwood Estates. Streets in the Dogwood Estates were named after trees, birds, and nature areas. They have a special group of names, of which pin oak is one. The pin oak has many short pinlike twigs that clutter the branches and can easily be identified. Pin Oak Drive was dedicated on July 20, 1964, in Ordinance 162-64. (Information is from the *Golden Nature Guide*.)

PINE CONE DRIVE (F7)

Pine Cone Drive was dedicated on February 17, 1987, in City Ordinance 2-87. It was part of the Pine Grove Subdivision. Part of West 44th Street (a 175-foot portion) was changed to Pine Cone Drive on January 19, 1987, in City Ordinance 10-87. From the city records it appears that West 44th Street had its name changed to Pine Cone Drive before Pine Cone Drive received its name. Elaine Koenig of Pine Cone Drive says this street was originally West 44th Street; however, it was very short then, and when Hyman builders came in, they changed it to Pine Cone Drive. Mrs. Koenig said a teacher from Dag Hammarskjold Elementary School told her that the whole area by Pine Cone Drive was full of pine trees. This area is located in the southern hills of the Parma community and is sometimes referred to as the secondary snow belt in the Cleveland area.

PINE FOREST DRIVE (F7)

This street was located in a wooded area that was full of pine trees. It was called the Pine Grove Subdivision. Pine Forest Drive was dedicated on February 17, 1987, in City Ordinance 2-87, along with Pine Cone Drive and Pine Oval.

PINEGROVE AVENUE (C2)

Pinegrove Avenue is located in a very appropriate place near the Metropark's Big Creek Parkway. This street was dedicated by the County Commissioners when Parma was only a township. The date of dedication was April 25, 1917. The owner was John P. Teufel and the developer was S. H. Kleinman Realty.

PINEHURST DRIVE (C7)

Pinehurst Drive is located in the Ames Road-Pleasant Valley Road area. It is off the main roads in a quiet residential area. It was dedicated on December 7, 1970, in Ordinance 352-70. It was part of the R. & O. Pinehurst Subdivision #1. As with most streets in this area, they were given good aesthetic names.

PINE OVAL (F7)

This street was dedicated on February 17, 1987, in City Ordinance 2-87. It was part of the Pine Grove Subdivision. This subdivision is located in a pine tree area on the hills of southern Parma.

PINEWOOD COURT (G3)

Pinewood Court was originally dedicated as West 11th Street. It was changed to Pinewood Court on October 2, 1978, in Ordinance 199-78. This attractively named street runs between Englewood Drive and Dartmoor Avenue.

PLAZA DRIVE (A3)

This street is a modern commercial drive. It was dedicated on October 4, 1976, in Ordinance 205-75. It is located off West 130th street, south of Snow Road on Parma's northwest side.

PLEASANT HILL DRIVE (B7)

Pleasant Hill Drive was originally dedicated as West 122nd Street on February 4, 1957. The name was changed on September 4, 1962, by the residents. Ella Greytak, a resident, said that since the street was on a slight hill, they felt Pleasant Hill would be a good name for their street. This street is also in the area of Pleasant Valley Road, which might have been a catalyst in naming this street. This is a very attractive street. Marvin Gross was the developer. Note: The Pleasant Hill Golf Course, in Chardon, was opened in 1963, a year after this street was dedicated, so this was not a factor in the naming of the street.

PLEASANT LAKE BOULEVARD (C-8)

At the center of the Pleasant Lake Apartments, this street is located off York Road south of Pleasant Valley Road. It was dedicated on December 6, 1963, in Ordinance 259-63, a Plat by the Northern Ohio Development Company. Much of this small and quite attractive lake is surrounded by this street. Its location in the Pleasant Valley Road area suggests how it may have received its name.

PLEASANT VALLEY ROAD (H-7)

The Pleasant Valley area was first surveyed in 1817 between Pearl Road and York Road. An Independence history book, through the courtesy of Dorothy Ones, stated that Pleasant Valley was extended from Brecksville Road to the River around 1913. The road itself, in Parma, was established in 1832. It was for many years just a dirt road. Pleasant Valley Road was extended to Bagley Road on April 19, 1954 (Ordinance 63-54). It is not known where the name came from, but it is believed to have come from either Independence or Valley View since this is where the picturesque valley stands out. Pleasant Valley Road, however, runs through a number of valleys from Broadview Road to York Road and gives many picturesque settings. This was especially true when it was a two-lane road prior to 1975. One thing is for sure: the name is perfect for the road.

PLEASANT VIEW DRIVE (J7)

Pleasant View Drive could have received its name because of its proximity with Pleasant Valley and the nearby view of Cleveland and the far west side. The street itself affords a very pleasant view. I am sure the residents would agree. Pleasant View Drive is located in the upper hills of southeastern Parma. It was dedicated on December 7, 1959, in City Ordinance 214-59. Bonny Builders were the developers.

POMONA DRIVE (A3)

Pomona Drive is part of the Western Heights Estates. As far as can be determined, this street was named after a suburb of Los Angeles, California. It was dedicated on September 19, 1966, in City Ordinance 349-66. The owners of the property were Norbert Milan and Sylvia Milan. The developer was the Patricia Development Company. Appropriately enough, this development is located in the far northwest area of Parma. This street, along with the others in the area, was named after western cities.

POMPANO DRIVE (F8)

Pampano Drive was named after Pampano Beach and city in Florida. This street was dedicated on August 8, 1987, in City Ordinance 183-87. A group of streets in Parma were named for Florida cities after a city official recommended it upon his return from a Florida vacation. This was a second of a group of streets named after Florida Cities. It all started in about 1960. Information was received from former Parma Mayor James Day.

POWERS BOULEVARD (D5)

Powers Boulevard was named after Thomas Powers, who was Clerk of Parma City Court for ten years. He retired in 1969. He was also Council President for six years and Councilman-at-large for four years. Along with Mark Lynett, he was credited with doing a lot of the preliminary work on Parma Community Hospital. He lived on Manhattan Avenue in Parma. Powers Boulevard was dedicated on September 15, 1958 (Ordinance 266-58). Powers Boulevard starts at Ridge Road and runs to Parma Community Hospital and Parma Municipal Court.

PRISCILLA AVENUE (F4)

Priscilla Avenue was dedicated on November 21, 1927. The developers were the Mayflower Properties and the Puritan Reality Company. This street was likely named after Priscilla Mullins of *The Courtship of Miles Standish*, a poem (1858) by Henry Wadsworth Longfellow. A number of other streets in this area took on the names of other people in the poem. Alden Avenue (John Alden) and Standish Avenue (Captain Miles Standish) are examples. Besides the above companies, might not the Snow family have been responsible for naming this street? (See Alden Avenue for further information.) (See picture 39.)

QUEENS HIGHWAY (B3)

In Parma Heights, Queens Highway was dedicated on October 4, 1929. It is believed to have been named with the Garden City Philosophy in mind. Along with other streets in Parma and Parma Heights, the developers would set up areas with English names in an attempt to create what we would call a Garden City. (Cleveland Heights and Shaker Heights are examples.) These communities would be exclusive communities for the upper middle class and upper class people. They could be identified by winding roads, lakes, golf courses, parks, and streets with English place names. Typical examples of this in the Parma area would be Parma Circle (Ridgewood Circle) and the former Greenbriar Community of Parma, north of Snow Road from Pearl Road to Big Creek Parkway. Queens Highway is in the Greenbriar area. This street was the continuance of Queens Highway in Parma Heights. It was dedicated in Parma on June 20, 1955. For those who might wonder if the Queens Highway might have been dedicated to the Blessed Virgin because of Nazareth Academy, I am afraid Nazareth Academy was founded in 1957, 28 years after the street was named. The above assumptions (Garden Cities theory) have some persuasive reasons behind them. See "H. A. Stahl, a Tribute." The builder, in Parma, then was Sunrise Builder of Forest City. Sam Miller was the developer.

Did you know that . . . .

The township of **Russell** took its name from the first settlers in the area, (1818) the Gideon Russell family. The township took the name of Russell in 1827.

OHIO PLACE NAMES by Larry L. Miller
University of Indiana Press, 1996

RALSTON DRIVE (E5)

Ralston Drive was dedicated on September 5, 1967, in Ordinance 315-67. This was Ridge Road Subdivision #2. The Ralston name still is a mystery. Could it be named after Bob Ralston, a popular organ player on Lawrence Welk's show at the time? If anyone has information on the naming of this street, please let the Historical Society know. None of the relatives of the developer had any information about the naming of this street. Historical figures with the name Ralston are: James Ralston, a Canadian lawyer of the 1920's, and William Ralston, an English scholar (1829 to 1889).

RANDOLPH DRIVE (E6)

This street was actually dedicated on December 5, 1966, in Ordinance 405-66. This is a partial street. It is the first street south off Regency Drive, east of Ridge Road, and it runs in the direction of Stearn's Farm. The developer could give no reason for giving the street this name except for aesthetic purposes. This street is named on the Plat maps.

RAVINE BOULEVARD (G3)

Ravine Boulevard was originally called South Park Boulevard East. It was dedicated as such on April 11, 1923, by the Township. It was named by Don Helwick, a developer. (See South Park Boulevard (East) for an interesting explanation). On October 22, 1956, in Ordinance 252-56, the name was changed by City Council to Ravine Boulevard. Both names were appropriate for this development, as the road runs around Quarry Creek Valley, which gives the neighbors in the area a nice view of the valley.

RAVENSWOOD DRIVE (C6)

Ravenswood Drive was dedicated on September 9, 1992, in Ordinance 198-92. It was called the Ravenswood Subdivision. A raven is a glossy black bird which is found in America, Northern Europe and Asia. Ancient people believed that evil spirits took the form of ravens. They are like large crows but are unique because of their size and glossy black feathers. Ravens are about 26 inches long. Edgar Allan Poe wrote "The Raven," a poem of grief and melancholy which became known throughout the world. The name Ravenswood gives a little mystery to this street. Actually the raven is just another bird; however, the way it spreads its wings, it seems it would like us to think it is much better than the ordinary bird. Then, again, we have a golf course in Ravenna, Ohio, called Ravenswoods Golf Course. However, this street is not named after the golf course. The developer did not know why this name was picked.

REDFERN ROAD (E3)

Redfern Road was dedicated on March 8, 1926. It was part of the Parmawood Development. Bingham-Priest Company was the developer. O. A. Priest and Roscoe Ewing were the officers. Research has not uncovered a tree by this name, and it is not too clear why the street was called Redfern. It is a nice sounding name, and it seems as though a red fern would be an interesting plant. The officials at the Holden Arboretum confirm that there is no such plant. This is really a unique name for a very attractive street. From the research done, it appears this name was given for aesthetic purposes only.

REGAL DRIVE (D6)

Regal Drive was dedicated on January 6, 1969, in Ordinance 397-68. According to Julius Paris, the developer, this name was given this street for aesthetic purposes. Regal refers to something that would be suitable for a king or something of notable excellence or magnificence. The name seems to fit the area well.

REGENCY DRIVE (D6)

Regency Drive was dedicated on September 5, 1967, in City Ordinance 315-67. This street was given this name for aesthetic purposes. It was named for the prestige it would give the area. A regent is one who governs, and a group of regents (governors) is called a regency. The name carries prestige with it because of the authority or power it represents.

REICHERT ROAD (C7)

Reichert Road was named after Roland Reichert, Mayor of Parma from 1936 to 1942 and from 1946 to 1949. Besides his 9 years as mayor, he was also a Parma municipal judge from 1962 to his death in 1965. He lived on South Canterbury Road. Reichert Road was dedicated on November 4, 1957, in Ordinance 306-57. Information came from former Mayor of Parma James Day. (See picture 50.)

RENO DRIVE (B3)

Reno is part of the Western Heights Estates. This street and other streets in the Western Heights Estates were all named after Western cities; they are appropriately named since this development is located on Parma's far northwest side. Reno Drive was dedicated on September 19, 1966, in Ordinance number 349-66. The Patricia Development Company was the company that did the development; Norbert Malin was president and Sylvia Malin was secretary. Slabe-MacKay were the Civil Engineers. Other streets in the development were Denver Drive, Tucson Drive, Pomona Drive, and Houston Drive.

RENWOOD DRIVE (D3)

Renwood Drive was dedicated on March 26, 1924, in Ridgewood Estates #2. H. A. Stahl was the developer who laid out the street. Mr. Stahl took most of the names for his streets from an English source. It is believed that he used the same source employed by the VanSweringen Brothers in laying out Shaker Heights. Though this name cannot be identified in any of these sources, it is believed that for some personal reason he gave this street this name. Could it have been a golf course since he was an ardent golfer? There is, however, no golf course in this area that has that name.

RICHARD DRIVE (B2)

Richard Drive was dedicated on September 20, 1954 (City Ordinance 198-54). It was named after Richard Miller, the son of Sam Miller, the developer for Forest City Enterprises. Information came from Plat 7711, Vol. 520 County Plat Book, and Sam Miller's office.

RIDGE ROAD (D2)

Ridge Road was first dedicated as a paved road on October 10, 1928. It was originally called Center Road because it ran through the center of Parma Township. It was a red brick road and according to Kubasek's *History of Parma*, "It was reported to be one of the finest pavements in Ohio." At the present time Ridge Road is Parma's "main road," bringing traffic from Cleveland to Parmatown Mall and then to residential areas. Ridge Road was named some time after 1874. In an 1874 map of Cleveland, the present day Ridge Road could not be found. What is really interesting is that what is now Denison Avenue, which runs along the ridge overlooking the Big Creek (Metroparks Zoo), was called Ridge Road. It was sparsely populated at the time and appeared to be on the ridge of today's zoo. It appears, for some reason, that this Ridge Road was changed to Denison Avenue and that another street, possibly Iona Street, took on the name Ridge Road. This was some time after 1874. Ridge Road in Parma eventually took its name from its Cleveland counterpart. Thus we have the reason for the name "Ridge Road" for our main street in Parma. Ridge Road became State Route 3 on August 20, 1947. In the early 1900's Ridge Road in some areas was known as the Cleveland-Rittman Pike. Information is from the Cuyahoga County Information Office. (See plat map, page 120, and pictures 29 and 32.)

RIDGEFIELD ROAD (D2)

This street was dedicated on December 18, 1919, when Parma was still a township. This was part of the Wooster Park Subdivision. The homes on Ridgefield Road have larger front yards and consist of both older and newer homes, giving a

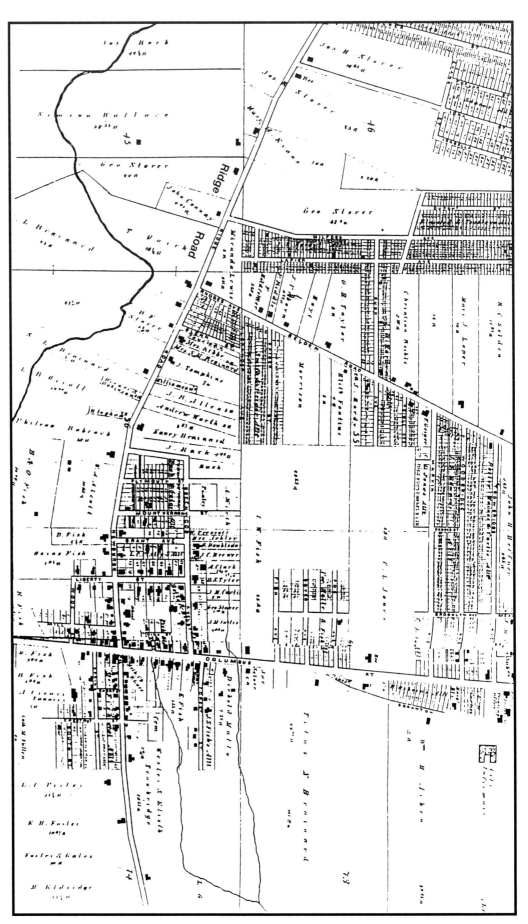

1874 PROPERTY–PLAT MAP OF RIDGE ROAD (DENISON AVENUE
AND NEWBURGH ROAD (HARVARD AVENUE)
AND COLUMBUS ROAD (LATER PEARL STREET, AND WEST 25TH STREET)

(See Ridge Road for information)

very good appearance. A unique "Fast Eddie's" restaurant is on the corner of Pearl and Ridgefield Avenue. Back in the 1950's, this restaurant used to be a "Bearden's" restaurant. This street probably received its name from its location. A number of streets around Ridge Road have the prefix "Ridge" in their names.

RIDGEWOOD AVENUE (D2)

Ridgewood Avenue was dedicated on September 13, 1919. It was part of the Ridgewood Garden Allotment. It was not part of the H. A. Stahl development as one might think but rather was the work of the Wooster Park Land Co. However, H. A. Stahl was secretary for the company. This was the early days of H. A. Stahl's involvement in Parma. Land owners were George and Minnie Friedrich, Emma Ball and W. L. Douglas. Ira Siegfried and Barbara Siegfried were also land owners. Of course the "Ridge" of Ridgewood was probably the result of its connection to Ridge Road.

RIDGEWOOD DRIVE (E5)

Ridgewood Drive was laid out by H. A. Stahl, the man who set up this whole area of Parma, the Ridgewood development, from Snow Road to Ridgewood Drive. Ridgewood Drive was dedicated on July 15, 1926. He also set up the Ridgewood Country Club and Golf Course. The Golf Course opened in July 1925. Earlier portions of Ridgewood Drive were called Bean Road (because of the bean farmers); Short Road, off Broadview Road; Valley View; and Axehandle (nickname) Road, which ran east off State Road. These names were changed on October 2, 1933 (Ordinance 145), as Ridgewood Drive found its way from Parma to Seven Hills. Information is from County Plat Maps and Kubasek's *History of Parma*. (See picture 2.)

RIDGEWOOD LAKES DRIVE (D5)

The location of this street gave it its name. The street is located on the northwest section of Ridge

Road and Ridgewood Drive, and it runs between the two Ridgewood Lakes. This street was dedicated at the request of H. A. Stahl on March 26, 1924, as part of Ridgewood Estate #9.

RIESTER AVENUE (F5)

This street was named after the last Chairman of the Board of Trustees for Parma Township. The Trustees were A. E. Riester (Chairman), J. D. Loder and A. F. Brown. They turned the township government over to the new Village government head, Parma's first mayor, John F. Goldenbogen, on January 1, 1925. Augustine E. Riester was a millionaire, according to a great nephew Richard Reising. He gave a lot of money to Parmadale. Mr. Riester and his wife had adopted two children from Germany. He owned a sheet metal business at West 25th and Clark Avenue. They lived in a home where St. Anthony's Church is now located. Later their home was used by Catholic Charities for a while as an infant home. Chairman Riester worked with H. A. Stahl in laying out Parma. By 1924, H. A. Stahl had sold over 6000 lots in Parma and had 4000 more to sell. Mr. Stahl set up the Parma Circle area and the Ridgewood Golf Course. Riester Avenue was dedicated on October 22, 1922. The developers of Riester Avenue were Helwick and Hopper. (Information is from *History of Parma* by Ernest R. Kubasek, page 111, and county plat maps.)

RIVER EDGE DRIVE (B2)

River Edge Drive (or Riveredge) was dedicated on September 3, 1957, in City Ordinance 212-57. This street is in the vicinity of Big Creek Parkway and probably gets its name from its location. The street was developed by Shelby Homes; they were responsible for homes in Cleveland for many years.

ROANOKE DRIVE (G4)

Roanoke Drive was dedicated on December 5, 1966, in Ordinance 424-66. This street was probably named after Roanoke Island in North Carolina. This was where the English tried a settlement in 1585 but failed. In 1587 they tried again and this is where and when Virginia Dare was born, the first child of English parentage to be born in America. In fact, Roanoke Island is in Dare County. Roanoke Island is located about 50 miles south of the Virginia border on the coastline. The city of Roanoke, Virginia, might also have been a catalyst in naming this street. The city of Roanoke has a population of 96,000. The fact that other streets in the area also carry historical names might also have been a factor in the naming of this street. There is also a street in Old Brooklyn by this name. This street was developed by Ambassador Homes (#1).

ROBERT STREET (G8)

County records indicate that this street was dedicated on June 9, 1955. It was dedicated by the land owners and developers Albert and Elizabeth Marusa. Albert named this street after his son Robert. Robert is now living in Tucson, Arizona, and is in the insurance business. Information came from Howard Marusa, Robert's stepbrother. There was also a dedication of December 17, 1962, in Ordinance 164-62, probably an extension date. (See Howard Street for further information.)

ROBINHOOD DRIVE (D6)

Robinhood Drive was dedicated on May 11, 1959, in Ordinance 88-59. Robinhood may have been a legendary figure or may have actually existed. Like Camelot, no one knows. This street was named after this legendary hero along with other streets in the area that took their names from the story of this man named Robinhood. (See King Richard Drive for further information.) The expression "Go around Robinhood's (Robinson's) barn to get to the front door" comes from this legendary figure. It means going out of your way to accomplish some simple task that could be done in a much simpler manner. It meant that Robinhood would go around

neighboring farm fields (Robinhood's Barn) to steal food for his men. Not the best way to make a living! (Information is from *Hog on Ice* by Charles Funk.)

ROCKSIDE ROAD (G3)

I guess Rockside Road is somewhat self-explanatory. Officially, according to the history received from the Henninger family, Rockside received its name from the quarries in Parma and Independence townships (Seven Hills). The Henninger, Buhl, Darrow and Kinzer properties are where many of the quarries were found. The stone from these quarries was used for building the Henninger home on Old Rockside Road and Broadview Road. The stone was also used for the Lake Erie break wall, the Ohio Erie Canal Locks, and was shipped to ports around the Great Lakes. There is only a small section of Rockside Road in Parma, but it is a very important section.

ROEDEAN DRIVE (C2)

This street was dedicated Roedean Drive in 1962. It was originally (1961) called Eaton Drive. It is part of the Fernhill Heights subdivision. With the help of residents and the help of Cuyahoga County library, the origin of this name was discovered. This street was named after an elite school for girls in Brighton, England, called Roedean School, located on Roedean Way (i.e., located directly south of London on the English Channel). This has been verified through residents and the internet at the Cuyahoga County Public Library. The reason for this credible assumption is the following: One resident said she heard that the developer renamed the street because of the Communist connection with the street's first name, Eaton. (There is a school in Berkshire, England, by the name of Eton also.) She also said that a store clerk told her that the name of her street was the same name as a school in England. A few years later, another resident said that she heard the developer renamed this street Roedean Drive after the school in England where he sent his daughter. A librarian with the county library, through the internet, showed a school in Brighton, England, called Roedean School on Roedean Way. No college, university or private school in this country could be found by that name (per the internet). This street is also located with a group of streets that have been named after institutions of learning, most of which are in England. The date of dedication was November 6, 1961, in City Ordinance 200-61.

ROEPER ROAD (E8)

Lester Roeper was police chief of Parma from 1945 to 1960. Roeper Road was named in his honor. This street was dedicated on April 16, 1962, in Ordinance 38-62. This information was confirmed by former Mayor James Day on 3-29-89.

ROMILLY OVAL (D6)

Romilly Oval was named after Milly Roob (Ro Milly). She was the mother of Ted Roob (our informant). She was married to Milton J. Roob (died 1963), who was construction superintendent for George Seltzer, one of the developers. Milly Roob lived in Parma most of her life. She died in March 1995. Romilly Oval was dedicated on July 3, 1961, in City Ordinance 131-61. Inadvertently, this street also carries the name of a historical person of whom little is known. His name is Samuel Romilly. He was a law reformer in England in the 1820's. The naming of this street says a lot about how streets can be named!

RONALD DRIVE (B7)

Ronald Drive was dedicated on October 2, 1958, in Ordinance 250-58. According to the developers, David Moskowitz and Robert Madow, this street was named after two of their children: Ronald Madow and Ronald Moskowitz.

ROSESIDE DRIVE (Fl)

Roseside was dedicated on April 20, 1918, and at first was thought to be named after one of the Henninger children, the property owners. This is what Carol Uhinck thought; her family also owned some of this property. But after a thorough check with the Henninger family, no child could be found with the name of Rose. Owners of the land were Roman Henninger, Edward Henninger and Nellie Henninger, and Anna Uhinck. Daleside Drive was also a street in this development which was thought to be named after another Henninger child, Dale Henninger. Again, no child in the Henninger family could be found with the name Dale. This is the same family who owned the 1849 home at the corner of Old Rockside and Broadview Road. Much research has been done on this development, but no leads have turned up. Woodway Avenue was also part of this development. The arrangement of these three streets makes a very attractive neighborhood, a park-like setting. Rosedale Avenue is the second street west of State Road off Brookpark Road. If anyone has information as to the naming of this street, please let the Historical Society know.

ROUSSEAU DRIVE (D6)

Rousseau Drive was dedicated on January 6, 1969 (Ordinance 397-68). According to Julius Paris, he named this street along with some others for the sound quality of the French name. Actually, the French philosopher Jean Jacques Rousseau was well known, and this street might be said to be named after him because of the popularity of his name. He believed that true religion consisted in the love for everything good and beautiful. Many people feel he didn't go quite far enough. Because of his belief, he could be said to be, in some way, in accord with Christianity, which believes that true religion consists in the love of God, who is everything good and beautiful. He lived from 1712 to 1778.

ROYAL RIDGE DRIVE (D6)

Royal Ridge Drive was dedicated on December 7, 1959 (Ordinance 212-59). This is part of the Seltzer-Wickman-Stormes development. It probably got part of its name from Ridge Road, inasmuch as many streets took part of their name from the main street close to them. (See Ridgefield Avenue, Ridgewood Avenue and Broadrock Avenue.)

ROYAL VIEW DRIVE (D6)

Royal View Drive was dedicated on November 3, 1965, in Ordinance 234-65. High View Drive was also dedicated in the same Sidney-Simon Subdivision #1. Both names for these streets appear to have been named for the esthetical value. After looking at this street, one could say the view is Royal. (See High View Drive.)

ROYCROFT DRIVE (D5)

This street was dedicated on March 26, 1924. The property was laid out by H. A. Stahl of the H. A. Stahl Properties. It was part of the Ridgewood Subdivision No 2. The Roycroft name comes from a unique furniture style or design. It is quite complicated because the Roycroft name comes from two men named Samuel and Thomas Roycroft, who started a printing business in the 17th century. This name was chosen by Elbert Hubbard in 1895 to honor these two men, not for a furniture store but rather for a printing company which Mr. Hubbard started himself so as to print his own material. He wanted to revive the printing art in this country and he did this, not only by his printed material but also by his own personal publications, magazines, biographical sketches of famous people and articles. It was only after he started his own bindery that the furniture business started to be profitable. A leather working shop for binding books led to leather furniture. Though Elbert Hubbard died in 1915 (he died on the *Lusitania* in 1915), a man named William Morris inspired the furniture business to the extent that Roycroft furniture made an important contribution to the growth of American arts and crafts design in this country. Nearly all Roycroft furniture is superbly made. Gustav Stickley also contributed to the total design of Roycroft furniture. So Roycroft Drive

was not only named after some of America's finest art crafted furniture but also after two famous printers, Samuel and Thomas Roycroft.

RUHR DRIVE (C8)

Ruhr Drive was dedicated on March 2, 1970, in Ordinance 396-69, along with Munich Drive and Vienna Drive. All these German-named streets are located around the German Central Farm off York Road. According to former Mayor James Day, this street was named after an industrial valley called the Ruhr Valley in Germany. Some of the major cities in this area are Essen, Koln (Cologne), and Dusseldorf. It is an area where steel is produced. This information was verified by Joe Holzer of the German Cultural Center in North Olmsted. This was the Richard Subdivision #9.

RUNNING BROOK DRIVE (C7)

Running Brook Drive was dedicated on July 7, 1980, in City Ordinance 114-79. It was part of the Black Forest Acres. This was a work of the Sunrise Development Company. It is a unique area located near the German Central Farm and Pleasant Valley Lake. Other streets in the area have names such as Fox Hollow Drive and Deer Run Trail, very picturesque names for a nice residential community.

RUSSELL AVENUE (E2)

This street was our most difficult street to identify, with the possible exception of Tuxedo Avenue. Russell Avenue was dedicated on September 19, 1908, by the Parma Township. Later the street was extended toward State Road in the State View Subdivision, and that part was dedicated on December 6, 1926. There have been six years of research and no substantial facts have been established. Margaret (Litz) Downs of Russell Avenue said the Kuchle family originally owned this land. The Edward Kuchle family was located on Lincoln Avenue in Parma. Mrs. Kuchle gave us the name of her sister-in-law, Eleanor Schuttenberg, who kept this type of information. Mrs. Schuttenberg, 80, said she has no idea how Russell got its name but that her grandfather owned the land where the street is now when she was a teenager. She is the last one in her family (1989). County records indicated that a Mr. Archie Ranney and Jennie Ranney had bought some of this land from a John Kaiser (west end of this property to State Road) and that a Frank M. Ranney presented his plan, Russell Avenue Plat, to the Parma Township at a hearing on February 2, 1908. Eventually it was dedicated on September 19, 1908. There is no information as to why this street was named Russell. It is worthwhile mentioning that a family named Russell lived on Cleveland's west side in 1874 and owned a large section of land there. William Russell was the owner. There does not appear to be any connection, however. All of the above, however, was mentioned because it is a part of the history of the street. Research will continue.

RUSTIC TRAIL (G5)

Rustic Trail is located at the top of Broadview Hill. It is a very attractive street as it slopes down the hill towards the west and the Quarry Creek Valley. It was dedicated on November 5, 1984, in Ordinance 115-84. Mr. William Hoislbauer I was the developer, and Fragapane Construction Company built the homes. Mr. Hoislbauer was born on August 23, 1902, and died in June 1989. Two other small circles in this development, William Circle and Holly Circle, were named after relatives of Mr. Hoislbauer. (See Holly and William Circles for further information.)

SAGAMORE ROAD (G7)

Sagamore Road was dedicated on October 22, 1956, in Ordinance 246-56 (County Plat book 166, page 32). The name Sagamore is a very popular name in northeast Ohio. There are eight streets, a hospital and a Summit County town that have this name. A national historical site called Sagamore Hill in Oyster Bay, New York, is where President Theodore Roosevelt was buried; the name's connection with Roosevelt may have made it popular at one time. The name Sagamore is also a name of a subordinate chief in the Algonquin Indian tribe. Frank Russo was the developer. It would seem the popularity of the name is the reason for the naming of this street as such.

ST. ANDREW'S DRIVE (F8)

St. Andrew's Drive was named after St. Andrew's Ukranian Church in the same area. It was dedicated on June 16, 1986, in City Ordinance 138-86. Al Rispo was the developer. An extension was added on March 18, 1991.

ST. PETERSBURG DRIVE (F8)

St. Petersburg Drive is located in the southern hills of Parma and is part of the second group of streets named for cities in Florida. It was during the 1960's and 1970's that these streets were laid out. The subject of retirement was becoming more of a reality for many people, and Florida was becoming a very popular place. It was also becoming a vacation paradise. When former Mayor James Day was Councilman-at-large during the 1960's, he suggested Florida names for streets after returning from a Florida vacation. St. Petersburg Drive was dedicated on October 2, 1978, in Ordinance 210-78 and was part of the so-called "Second Florida Estates." Sunrise Development Company was the developer.

SALISBURY DRIVE (D4)

This street takes its name from a very small cathedral town in England called Salisbury. It is located about 20 miles northwest of the sea coast town of Southampton. Salisbury is largely known for its Salisbury Cathedral, which was finished in 1258. Salisbury Drive was dedicated on March 26, 1924, at the request of H. A. Stahl, the developer. (See pictures of homes on Salisbury Drive, built in the 1920's, pictures 36, 37, 38.) (For further information, see "H. A. Stahl, A Tribute" and "The Garden City" in this book.)

SANDPIPER DRIVE (Private) (G2)

Sandpiper Drive was developed between 1974 to 1977. It is named after a North American bird that is generally referred to as a shore bird or marsh bird. It is identified by its walk. When it walks it typically teeters up and down in a very interesting fashion.

SANDY HOOK DRIVE (E7)

Sandy Hook Drive was dedicated on April 16, 1962, in City Ordinance 38-62. This was part of the Woodbury Hills subdivision. The New Jersey coast has a public beach five miles long called Sandy Hook. Gateway National Recreation Park is located in this area and has an historical lighthouse called the Sandy Hook Lighthouse, which was built in 1764. It was used by the British in the Revolutionary War. It is located on the coast of Monmouth County, New Jersey (See Monmouth Drive). There is also a little town in central Virginia called Sandy Hook. Though we do not have verification as to the naming of this street, it appears that New Jersey's Sandy Hook Beach and Lighthouse could have been factors in the naming of Sandy Hook Drive.

SANFORD DRIVE (F8)

This street was named after a city in Florida, northeast of Orlando and about 30 miles from the Atlantic Ocean. Sanford has a population of 32,387, according to the 1990 census. This street was dedicated on June 16, 1986, in Ordinance 138-86. This street and other streets in the area were named after Florida cities during the 1970's and 1980's. This street

is located just behind St. Andrew's Church and St. Peter and Paul Cemetery off Hoertz Road. (See Winter Park Drive for further information.)

SAPPHIRE COURT (C7)

Sapphire Court was named for the birthstone of the builder's wife. Her name was Sandra Semra Simich. The street was dedicated on February 24, 1997, in Ordinance 389-96. Minor George was the developer, and Michael Deacon was the realtor. (For more information see Semra Circle.)

SARASOTA DRIVE (E7)

Sarasota Drive was dedicated on August 4, 1966, in Ordinance 295-66. It is one of the streets developed in the so-called "Florida Estates." There is a city in Florida, about 30 miles south of Tampa-St. Petersburg called Sarasota. This street was named after this city. (See Winterpark Drive for further information on the naming of this street.)

SASSAFRAS DRIVE (E7)

Sassafras Drive was named after "one of the most famous of all early American trees," the sassafras tree, according to Ernest Kubasek in his *History of Parma*. This was one of the original trees in Parma before the area was settled. The street was dedicated by city council on January 6, 1969, in Ordinance 397-68. Information is from *History of Parma* by Ernest R. Kubasek, and Parma City Hall files.

SCARLET OAK LANE (C8)

Scarlet Oak Lane is located in the Dogwood Estates. Bonny Builders were the developers. It was dedicated on February 20, 1967. The scarlet oak tree is noted for the brilliant color of its autumn leaves. The streets in the Dogwood Estates were named after trees, birds, and nature areas. The developer said he chose names that he felt people would find interesting and attractive.

SCHWAB DRIVE (B7)

This street was named after the Schwab family of Schwab Electric. Lou Schwab was the founder of Schwab Electric and the husband of Luelda Gehring Schwab Barton. His wife, Luelda, was a Krather from Brooklyn and has an interesting background of her own. Luelda Avenue was named after her. Schawb Drive was dedicated on April 15, 1957, in Ordinance 63-57. Lou Schwab was born in 1899 and died in 1948. The Schwab family owned a farm on the land where this street is now located. Information is from Parma City Hall and Luelda Barton. (For further information, see Luelda Avenue.)

SEDGEWICK AVENUE
West 29th Street (F3)

This street does not exist at this time. However, this name throws a light on the Garden City concepts that the VanSweringen brothers had for Shaker Heights and that Don Helwick and H. A. Stahl appear to have had for Parma. What was once Sedgewick Avenue is now West 29th Street. The name the Van Sweringen brothers gave the syndicate which they formed to set up their model city, Shaker Heights, was Sedgwick Land Company. (A slight difference in spelling would not have been unusual in the early 1900's.) Don Helwick named what is now West 29th street as "Sedgewick Avenue." Sedgewick Avenue was accepted (dedicated) by the County Commissioners on June 2, 1923. However, this street was changed to West 29th Street on May 31, 1932, to better identify the house numbers (Ordinance 57-1932). Just to the east of Sedgewick Avenue was Malvern Avenue (now West 33rd Street, changed at the same time for the same reason). Malvern is another name from Shaker Heights (Malvern Road). Both Mr. Helwick and Mr. Stahl were residents of the Shaker Heights/Cleveland Heights area, and there are strong indications they had in mind to develop Parma into another model Garden City. The Depression destroyed their plans, and, you might say, their lives. Though a multi-millionaire, H. A. Stahl

lost everything in the Depression, and it is reported he worked for the county the last couple years of his life. He died in 1930 of heart failure. (See "H. A. Stahl, A Tribute" and "A Man With a Plan" (about Mr. Helwick) in this book for further information.

SELWICK DRIVE (D6)

Selwick Drive was taken from the names of Seltzer and Wickman of the Seltzer, Wickman and Stormes Developing Company. The street was dedicated on May 20, 1957, in Ordinance 113-57. Information is from former Mayor James Day.

SEMRA CIRCLE (C7)

Semra Circle was named for the builder's wife; her name was Sandra Semra Simich. The builder is Thomas Simich. Semra Circle was dedicated on February 24, 1997, in Ordinance 389-96. A little information about Semra: She is a registered nurse at the Cleveland Clinic. She and Tom have two children: Chad and Jennifer. Minor George was the developer, and Mike Deacon was the realtor on this street.

SEQUOIA DRIVE (E7)

Sequoia Drive is part of the Woodbury Hills Development. It was dedicated on April 16, 1962, in Ordinance 38-62. A sequoia is a redwood tree in California. The Sequoia National Forest (Park) is located on the western slopes of the Sierra-Nevada Mountain Range in Central California. Interestingly enough, it was not discovered by the settlers until the mid 1800's. The name itself comes from a Cherokee Indian (Sequoia 1770-1840), who invented an alphabet for his tribe, a major step forward for the Cherokee Indians. This street is located in a beautiful wooded area; this may have been the catalyst in the naming of this street. Interesting note: A Sequoia redwood tree named Howard Libby stands 367 feet high, the height of a thirty-story building! (Information is from *Every Day Words* by Allan Wolk, page 60.)

SESQUICENTENNIAL DRIVE (A6)

This park street was named by Mayor John Petruska in 1976 for Parma's 150 years (1826 to 1976) as a township. The city of Parma celebrated its 70th birthday in 1994 as a city-village. On December 15, 1924, Parma was incorporated as a village.

SHARON DRIVE (B2)

Sharon Drive was dedicated on June 20, 1955, in Ordinance 144-55. It is located within a group of biblically named streets. They either were named after people or places in the Bible, or they were named for children who had biblical names. Sharon Drive seems to follow this pattern. There is a fertile plain that occupies the central region of Palestine on the Mediterranean sea coast called the Plain of Sharon. It varies in width from 6 to 12 miles from Joppa to Carmel. This appears to be the reason for naming this street as it is. Some of the other streets in the area were named after children of the developers or builders; however, this street could not be identified with anyone. Some of the other streets in this development are Naomi Drive, Deborah Drive, Aaron Drive and Abraham Drive–all biblical names.

SHENANDOAH OVAL (G6)

Shenandoah Oval was dedicated on April 7, 1980, in Ordinance 166-79. It is part of the Green Belt Subdivision, the so-called "Gettysburg Estates." It is located off Broadview Road north of Pleasant Valley Road. The Shenandoah River runs through Virginia and West Virginia into the Potomac River at Harper's Ferry. The Battle of Bull Run was fought in the Shenandoah Valley about 40 miles from Harper's Ferry. See Sherman Drive for related information.

SHERATON DRIVE (F3)

Sheraton Drive was dedicated on June 23, 1922. (Information is from City Hall.) A family by the name of Shermer (aka Sherman) owned the land before they sold it to the developers. Nothing was confirmed after research was done on the Sheraton name. Could this street be named after the owner, or could the owner's name be a catalyst in the naming of this street? If someone has information on the naming of this street, please contact The Parma Area Historical Society.

SHERIDAN DRIVE (G6)

Sheridan Drive was dedicated on December 2, 1968, in Ordinance 396-68. It was named after a Civil War general by the name of Philip H. Sheridan. He was famous at the battles of Perryville, Shenandoah and the Appomattox Campaign. This is part of the so-called "Gettysburg Estates." See Sherman Drive for further information on this street.

SHERMAN DRIVE (G6)

Sherman Drive is part of the Charles Subdivision #2 or what is commonly known as the "Gettysburg Estates." These Estates are located west off Broadview Road between Chestnut Drive and Pleasant Valley. Sherman Drive was dedicated on December 2, 1968, in Ordinance 398-68. Former Parma Mayor James Day had suggested these names after he came back from a visit to Gettysburg, Pennsylvania. (Sherman was the Union General famous for his march to the sea, in which Atlanta was burned in the process, in May and June of 1864.)

SHERWOOD DRIVE (G6)

Sherwood Drive is located in the so-called "Robinhood Estates." There is a Sherwood Forest Center in England located about 20 miles north of Nottingham, England. This is part of the area where Robinhood allegedly operated. In Parma this street is actually part of the Parmaview Estates Subdivision and was dedicated on May 11, 1959, in Ordinance 88-59. (Developers were G. Kiss and S. Miller.)

SHILOH CIRCLE (G6)

Shiloh Circle was dedicated on July 3, 1973, in Ordinance 11-73. It is part of the Gettysburg Estates off Broadview Road, north of Pleasant Valley. Shiloh was a battlefield in the Civil War. It was located on the Tennessee River east of Memphis. For a related discussion, see Sherman Drive.

SIERRA OVAL (D7)

Sierra Oval was dedicated on July 3, 1961, in Ordinance 136-61. Since this street is located in the Dogwood Estates where the streets are named after birds, trees, and nature areas, can one think of a greater nature area than the Sierra Nevada Mountain Range in California? Some of the greatest trees in the country are located on the western slopes of this range. Let us not forget the great Sierra Club either.

SKYLARK DRIVE (B7)

This street was renamed Skylark Drive on September 4, 1962, in Ordinance 104-62 by the residents. The original name was West 118th Street. According to Betty Kruse, a resident in the area, the unusual number of residents who owned Skylark cars was the catalyst for naming this street. The street was originally named West 118th Street and dedicated as such on May 5, 1958, in Ordinance 124-58. This development was called the Yorkland subdivision by Robert Madow and David Moskowitz.

SLEEPY HOLLOW DRIVE (A7)

Sleepy Hollow Drive received its name on September 4, 1962, in Ordinance 104-62. It was originally called West 123rd Street when it was dedicated by City Council on September 2, 1958, in Ordinance 250-58 (as requested by the developer, Marvin Gross). People in the community decided on the change and Council approved it on September 4, 1962, in City Ordinance 104-62. The only reason residents give for this name is that they liked the name. Remember the Headless Horseman, Sleepy Hollow, and Tarrytown, New York?

SNOW ROAD (F3)

Snow Road was named after the Clifford and Ann Snow family. Norma (Snow) Huey tells us that the Snow family farm was on State Road where Snow Road now intersects. However, when the family farm was there, there was no Snow Road. It seems that Clifford would lead the cows to pasture down a path toward what now is West 54th Street, and that path became what is now Snow Road. A path of a few hundred feet became a major thoroughfare cutting through the western part of Cuyahoga County. After Clifford's wife, Ann, died, he and his daughter, Marion, moved to Colorado (in 1942) where she is living now. The street Marioncliffe Drive was named after him and his daughter. The Snow Family first moved to Parma in 1834. Clifford is a descendant of the Pilgrims of Plymouth Rock. (See Genealogy in Parma Historical Library.) The last of the Snow family to live in Parma (5933 State Road) was Clifford Snow. He left in 1971. Information is from the County Plat records, Vol. 80, page 22. The original part of Snow Road (State Road to West 54th Street) was dedicated on November 8, 1922. Snow Road was not extended to Rockside until the mid 1950's.

SOMIA DRIVE (F4)

Somia Drive was named after Somia Aboukire, the wife of the builder, Charles Aboukire. Mr. Aboukire's assistant was Tony Giraldo, who was involved in building the homes on Somia Drive. Somia, herself, was a member of the prominent George family of Parma (Minor George's sister). Somia Drive was dedicated on May 1, 1961 (Ordinance 58-61). (See picture 26.)

SOUTH CANTERBURY ROAD (D4)

South Canterbury Road runs southwest from Ridgewood Circle to Ridgewood Drive to

Parmatown. Many of the homes on South Canterbury Road were built in the 1920's and are exceptional examples of Garden City architecture. (See pictures 14, 15, 16, 19 and 35.) South Canterbury Road was dedicated on March 26, 1924. H. A. Stahl was the developer. South Canterbury Road was to continue into what is now Parmatown (see plat map on page 22, the Douglas Circle Development). (Also see Canterbury Road for further information.)

SOUTHINGTON DRIVE (D4)

Southington Drive (the eastern half) was dedicated on October 22, 1924, in the Ridgewood Estates no. 6. The western half was dedicated on March 17, 1924, in the Ridgewood Estates no. 8. It is felt that H. A. Stahl, who developed Parma's Ridgewood Circle area, developed this community with the idea of developing a Garden City. It appears he applied all the ideas in Parma that were used in setting up Shaker Heights, that is, the Garden City philosophy. Included were the winding roads, lakes, green areas, parks and a golf course. The street names were taken from Shaker Heights streets or taken from the same English source from which the Shaker Heights streets were named, the Garden Cities of England in the 1920's. H. A. Stahl lived in Shaker Heights in the 1920's and had an office at Cedar and Coventry Roads. (See in this book "H. A. Stahl, A Tribute" for further information.) This street runs from West 54th Street through the Parma Circle area to Westminster Drive on Parma's far west side. The presence of brick homes gives this street a very attractive appearance. (See picture 20.) Southington in early English means "a southern town settled by a group of people" or a tribal southern town. (See *Place Names of the English Speaking World* by C. M. Matthews, page 37.)

SOUTH LINDEN LANE (A8)

South Linden Lane differs from the other Linden Lanes (Linden Lane, North, East and West) in that it is a private road and is not connected with the others; it has its own entrance off Pleasant Valley Road. All the other Linden Lanes are connected. According to Mary Lou Maderka, a resident of South Linden Lane, South Linden Lane is a private street and residents moved on the streets about 1950. She said that South Linden Lane was connected to North Linden Lane at one time until Millerwood Lane was constructed. From our research it appears to be the only private street in Parma with private homes. (For more information on this street see Linden Lane.)

SOUTH PARK BOULEVARD (G3)

South Park Boulevard was dedicated on April 11, 1923, as part of Exeter Park Allotment by developer Don Helwick. (Exeter is the name of a famous English Benedictine Monastery where St. Boniface was trained before leaving for Germany on his mission work. Exeter is also a name of a street in Cleveland Heights.) Wellington Park Allotments was another development involving South Park Boulevard. It appears that H. A. Stahl and Don Helwick had some great plans for Parma. While H. A. Stahl was working on the Parma Circle area, Mr. Helwick was working on the South Park Boulevard Area. He called the boulevard running along the west side of the Quarry Creek "South Park Boulevard West" and the Boulevard running along the east side of Quarry Creek "South Park Boulevard East" (now Ravine Boulevard). In Parma, South Park Boulevard does not really fit the location since it is on the west side of the park or what is called today Quarry Creek. Mr. Helwick, it seems, picked the name South Park Boulevard from Shaker Heights where South Park Boulevard has a reputation as a home for the elite. It seems he had intended to use the Quarry Creek area as a park, and his plans were to develop homes on both sides of the park (as is the situation in Shaker Heights with North and South Park Boulevards). It appears these two streets would have run the length of the park (to Grantwood Drive). As an interesting side note, the Cleveland Metroparks made an attempt to buy Quarry Creek in 1917, but land owners and the

Metroparks couldn't come to an agreement financially. Later, on October 22, 1956, in Ordinance 252-56, South Park Boulevard West was changed to South Park Boulevard, and South Park Boulevard East was changed to Ravine Boulevard. Some of the above information is from Claudia Helwick, daughter-in-law of Don Helwick. (For further information see articles "A Man With a Plan" and "Quarry Creek, a Forgotten Tributary" in this book.) (See picture 46.)

SOUTH TAMARACK DRIVE (E8)

South Tamarack Drive was originally dedicated West 46th Street on August 4, 1966 (Ordinance 294-66), and the residents had it changed to South Tamarack Drive on September 5, 1967, in Ordinance 312-67. Tamarac (note spelling difference) is the name of a small suburb of Ft. Lauderdale, Florida. There is no *South* Tamarack (Tamarac) in Florida. The "South" is apparently referring to its location here in Parma, south of Tamarack Drive.

SPRAGUE ROAD (D8)

Sprague Road was named after Milton Sprague. He was born in Parma in 1839 but received his education in Berea, and he also taught school in Berea. He was principal of Union Elementary School in Berea from 1872 to 1882. He bought the Sprague Carriage shop on the corner of Rocky River Drive and Bridge Street in Berea in the late 1800's. Records indicated that it burned down in 1903. He was a charter member of the Berea Chamber of Commerce when it was founded in 1887. According to the Berea Historical Society, an 1874 map also showed that a D. Sprague owned property near where Sprague Road intersects Pearl Road. The earliest date of dedication on record was on July 20, 1965. Sprague Road must have been there long before that.

SPRINGDALE AVENUE (D2)

Springdale Avenue was part of the Forest Lawn Subdivision and was dedicated on April 25, 1917.

This street is located in the Evergreen Lake area. This aesthetically named street has quite an appropriate name for this very natural area.

SPRING GARDEN ROAD (D3)

Spring Garden Road was part of the Tuxedo Garden Allotments and was dedicated on January 12, 1923. This street gives evidence of the Garden City philosophy of this time. The developer was Frank Johnson. This was developed at the time when H. A. Stahl and Don Helwick were setting up what might be called the Garden City idea for Parma. Mr. Johnson's Allotment was immediately north of H. A. Stahl's Development. (See "H. A. Stahl, A Tribute" and "The Garden City" in this book for related discussion.)

STANBURY ROAD (D4)

This is part of the H. A. Stahl Ridgewood (No. 3) Development. This street was dedicated on December 12, 1923, along with Wainstead Drive and Ivandale Drive. Stanbury Drive is located in an upper middle class area in a very attractive location. It appears that H. A. Stahl applied many of the ideas in Parma that were used in setting up Shaker Heights, Ohio; that is to say, the Garden City philosophy. Included were winding roads, lakes, parks and a golf course. The street names were taken from Shaker Heights streets or taken from the same English source from which the Shaker Heights streets were named: the English directories of the 1920's. H. A. Stahl lived in Shaker Heights in the 1920's and had an office at Cedar and Coventry Roads. (See in this book "H. A. Stahl, A Tribute" for further information.) According to *Place Names the English Speaking World* by C. M. Matthews, the suffix "bury" means stronghold, which was added to many city names since most cities in the early years of England were fortresses. In early England "Stan" meant "Stony." So Stanbury would mean a stony stronghold or fort. There is an important house in England called Stansteadbury. "Stead" in early England was used to stress the prefix. Home is more emphatic when used with stead: "Homestead." Information is from *Place Names of the English Speaking World* by C. M. Matthews, pages 39 and 62.

STANDISH AVENUE (D4)

Standish Avenue was dedicated on November 21, 1927. It is believed that this street and other streets in this area were named after the settlers in Longfellow's *The Courtship of Miles Standish*. They were Captain Miles Standish (Standish Avenue), Pricilla Mullin (Pricilla Avenue), and John Alden (Alden Drive). The companies involved were the Mayflower Properties Company and the Puritan Realty Company. The Snow family (from which Snow Road got its name) was related to John Alden (as can be seen in the genealogy of the family at the Parma Historical Library), and they lived in this area at the time the street was dedicated. It has not been determined whether the Snow family had any influence in the naming of these streets. The Snow family's name does not appear to be involved in these companies and the present day family has no knowledge of their involvement. (See picture 40.)

STANFIELD DRIVE (F5)

Stanfield Drive was dedicated on May 4, 1927. It was named after a dentist who became the mayor of Parma in 1926. He was Richard F. Stanfield. He was also one of the first members of council of the Village of Parma. Parma became a village on December 15, 1924. According to city records, part of Stanfield Drive was originally Overlook Drive and was changed to Stanfield Drive in 1932 in Ordinance 55-32.

STARY DRIVE (E7)

This is not an aesthetically named street; rather, it was named after a Parma Mayor, Lawrence Stary, who served two years as mayor from 1950 to 1952. Stary Drive was dedicated on November 16, 1964, in Ordinance 245-64; it was part of the Forestbrook Subdivision. Information is from former Mayor James Day and City Hall records. Part of West 38th Street was changed to Stary Drive on September 5, 1967, in Ordinance 295-67.

STATE ROAD (F2)

State Road became a county road in 1817. State Road is reported to have had residents on it in 1825, when a family by the name of Beal moved there from Royalton, Ohio. They were Abner and Jane Shepherd Beal. In 1835, according to county records, State Road was a private plank road. State Road became a State-responsible road in 1831. After 1906, part of State Road was known as West 35th Street. In the Brooklyn area, people never quite got used to calling State Road West 35th Street. The first public street car (the Dinky), with William McDiarmid as its motorman, came down State Road in 1915. State Road became State Route 94 on August 20, 1947. Some will remember the Soap Box Derby races when Parma was the guest for the Regional Soap Box Derby races held on State Road Hill in 1960. (Information on county roads is from the County Office and from the *History of Parma* by Ernie Kubasek, pages 55 and 148.) (See picture 39.)

STAUNTON DRIVE (G4)

Staunton Drive commemorates a town in Virginia. Staunton, Virginia, was located in an area where many Civil War battles took place. It is located near the West Virginia border. Staunton Drive was dedicated on December 1, 1964, in Ordinance 271-64, one hundred years after the Civil War. This street is located in the Gettysburg Estates. (See picture 41.)

STORMES DRIVE (D8)

This street was named after June Stormes, Secretary to the Planning Commission of the city of Parma in the 1950's. This street was dedicated on March 23, 1959, in Ordinance 51-59. Information is from former Mayor James Day and Parma City Hall.

STRATFORD DRIVE (C4)

Stratford Drive was dedicated by the township of Parma on March 26, 1924. It was part of H. A. Stahl's plan in laying out Parma Circle. He used the names of English towns for the streets. Stratford is a town located in central England. It is called Stratford-upon-Avon and is located about 75 miles northwest of London. Stratford is also a northern section of the city of London. For further information see "H. A. Stahl, A Tribute" in this book.

STUMPH ROAD (B3)

Stumph Road was named after John and Catherine Stumph (Stumpf), who owned the land in 1852, east of the area where Stumph Road is now located. However, the 1892 map shows that the Stumph family owned a large area of land where Stumph Road is now located. Other family owners in 1892 were: John Stumph Jr., Henry Stumph, Henrich Stumph, Kate Stumph and Daniel Stumph. It might be mentioned here that the Stumph family originally spelled their name Stumpf. On November 6, 1972, Ordinance 203-72 renamed part of Stumph Road from Brookpark Road to Snow Road as Chevrolet Boulevard. The west side of Chevrolet Boulevard is the area where the family owned most of their property. (Informants were Marie Sipple of Lorain and Dianna Schroeder, both of the Stumpf family.)

SUNDERLAND DRIVE (D4)

Sunderland Drive was dedicated on November 23, 1921, at the request of developer H. A. Stahl. This street runs between North Canterbury Road and Ackley Road, east of Ridge Road. It seems to have secured its name from the English town Sunderland, which is located on England's North Sea coast. Originally, the word "Sunderland" was used to describe a piece of property that is located some distance from the main property of the owner. For further information see the articles "H. A. Stahl, A Tribute" and "The Garden City" in this book. (Information is from *Place Names of the English*

Speaking World by C. M. Matthews, page 87; a Map of England by AAA; and Cuyahoga County Plat Maps at the County Administration Building.)

SUNHAVEN OVAL (F7)

This street was dedicated on January 15, 1962, in Ordinance 3-62 at the request of Bonny Builders. It is located in an area where streets are named after Florida cities and the sun. This street is located on a southern ridge (or the high country) of Parma.

SUNRAY DRIVE (H3)

This street was dedicated on July 5, 1960, in city Ordinance 131-60; it is part of the John Basile Subdivision. It was dedicated along with Decker Drive in the same area. Julius Paris named the street, according to developer Al Rispo. This is another street named aesthetically.

SUNRISE OVAL (D6)

Sunrise Oval was dedicated on January 5, 1962, in city Ordinance 3-62 at the request of Bonny Builders. Like Sunhaven Oval, this street was also located in an area where the streets were named after Florida cities and the sun. This is quite a positive approach in naming a street!

SUN VISTA DRIVE (D6)

Sun Vista Drive was dedicated as part of the Vista Ridge Estates on July 16, 1979, in city Ordinance 105-79. Sunrise builders were the developers. This development has many interesting and attractive names such as Eventide Drive and Night Vista Drive. The names are beautiful but strictly aesthetic.

TALBOT DRIVE (D5)

Talbot Drive was dedicated on December 5, 1966, in Ordinance 405-66. Though this is a fairly common name and should be easy to identify, it has been one of the most difficult names to identify with a person. Everyone now living who might have had a hand in naming this street could not tell us whom this street was named after. So we do not have an answer to this problem. I will, however, give a few notable people in history who have had this name. Talbot was the prominent Norman name of early England. There is a home that Catholic Charities operates called Matt Talbot. There was a famous Duke of Shrewsbury, England, called Charles Talbot (1660-1718). There was an English physicist, William Talbot (1800-1877), who taught at Harrow (see Harrow Drive), Trinity and Cambridge University. When a dog is used in heraldry, it is usually called a Talbot, or hunting dog.

TAMARACK DRIVE (F7)

Tamarack Drive is part of the State/Sprague Subdivision and was dedicated on August 4, 1966, in Ordinance 294-66. The developer was Stabe/MacKay. This is part of the so-called "Second Florida Estate." Tamarac is a suburban town near Fort Lauderdale, Florida. The reason for the difference in spelling (k) is not known. It might be interesting to note here that there is a famous golf course called Tamarack Golf Club in Naperville, Illinois, 30 miles southwest of Chicago. Could this street name have been spelled with a "k" on the end inadvertently, possibly, or could this street be named after the golf course? I doubt it. For further information on this street, see Winterpark Drive.

TAMIAMI DRIVE (G8)

Tamiami Drive (not Tamiami Trail as it was called in Florida) was dedicated on April 17, 1961. It seems Councilman-at-large James Day, soon to be Mayor in 1962, had just come back from vacation in Florida and he had suggested that names of Florida cities and places be given to new streets.

TANGLEWOOD LANE (D8)

Tanglewood Lane was dedicated on January 17, 1995, in Ordinance 209-94. It is part of the Pine Tree Development by Richard MacKay and William DeGraeve. This street and the others were all named after golf courses. Tanglewood golf course is located in Chagrin Falls, Ohio. Interesting note: Mr. MacKay tells us that in this development there is an oak tree called the Moses Oak because it is believed to have been here even prior to Moses Cleaveland's arrival. The tree has a plaque identifying it.

TERRACE COURT (C6)

In the original plans Terrace Court was to be called Holy Family Court (because of its proximity to Holy Family Parish on York Road). It appears there were objections to this name so the name Terrace was given. This name is also appropriate since the street is built on a little terrace which drops off behind the homes on the south side. Information is from Duane Whittenberger, a resident on the street. This street was dedicated on June 20, 1960, in City Ordinance 122-60.

THEOTA AVENUE (D2)

Theota Avenue is the location of the first settlement of Europeans in Parma. According to Dr. Dudley Fay (1989), Theota Avenue was named after a daughter of the J. R. Teufel family, who owned land near the Fay family. The Fays, the first settlers in Parma, owned the land just east of the Ridge–Pearl Roads intersection, and the Teufel family owned the land just west of that intersection. Theota Avenue continues through the intersection into the area of the Fays' farm on the east side of the intersection. Theota Avenue was dedicated on July 3, 1917.

THOREAU DRIVE (E6)

Thoreau Drive was dedicated on January 6, 1969, in Ordinance 397-68. The developer, Julius Paris, had quite a liking for French names and gave his streets French names for aesthetic reasons. A relative of Mr. Paris helped him pick the names, and sometimes they would pick poets or writers. There was an American writer named Henry David Thoreau, who lived from 1817 to 1862.

THORNCLIFF BOULEVARD (G6)

Thorncliff Boulevard was originally dedicated as Musso Boulevard. It was named after Frank Musso, the developer, who had the street dedicated Musso Boulevard on October 22, 1956, in Ordinance 246-56. The name was changed to Thorncliff Boulevard on December 7, 1959, in Ordinance 217-59. It is now part of the Gettysburg Estates. It runs along the cliff of Quarry Creek. This is quite a scenic view for the homes in this area. Information on dedication is from County Book 166, page 30, and from Parma City Hall.

THORNTON DRIVE (D3)

This street was dedicated on September 3, 1920 (Plat Map Vol. 76, page 4). The name was requested by H. A. Stahl, developer and Shaker Heights Resident. Part of Thornton was originally called Homestead Drive, west of Ridge Road, but because of the similarity between Homestead and Hampstead, City Council changed the name to Thornton on December 12, 1933, in Ordinance 158. Stahl, the developer, named many of his streets after English place names. The name Thornton comes from the Thorn-ton, a place with a thorn hedge. That is why the name was used so much, because people used to use this hedge for farms and homes. Information is from *Place Names of the English Speaking World* by C. M. Matthews. For further information see: "H. A. Stahl, a Tribute" in this book.

TIEDEMAN ROAD (Cl)

Tiedeman Road is named after the Hanus Tiedeman Family. Their home still stands on Tiedeman Road in the city of Brooklyn. They had a large family and a large home. The home

was built in 1860. In Parma, Tiedeman Road is very short. It runs between Brookpark Road and Hauserman Road. Tiedeman Road was dedicated by the county on September 21, 1954 (Vol. 146, page 42 - 2nd Floor County Administration Building). Parma, it seems, never had this as a dedicated road before 1954.

TORRINGTON AVENUE (E2)

Torrington Avenue was part of the Torrington Park Development. Developers were Elworthy and Helwick. Don Helwick was a resident of Shaker Heights and named many of his streets after Shaker Heights streets, or the same source the Van Sweringen brothers got their names for Shaker Heights streets, and that was from a Garden City Directories of England. In the early 1920's, Mr. Helwick seemed to have in mind for Parma a community of middle to upper middle class residents, but the Great Depression ruined his plans. There is a Torrington Road in Shaker Heights that runs near the Shaker Heights Country Club. Torrington Avenue was dedicated on August 20, 1924.

TRACY TRAIL (C6)

Tracy Trail was dedicated on May 20, 1957, in Ordinance 107-57. This street was named for the Safety Director of Parma, Walter Tracy. Walter was on the Planning Commission and was Recreation Director during his many years of public service. Information is from former Mayor of Parma James Day.

TREVOR LANE (D6)

Trevor Lane was dedicated on May 20, 1957, in Ordinance 113-57. This is the only street in Parma that carries the full name of the person it was named after. The man's name is Trevor Lane. When the builders, Seltzer-Wickman-Stormes, were laying out their development, they named this street after Ben Stormes' father-in-law, Trevor Lane. This information was received from Leonard Lane, son of Trevor Lane and brother-in-law of Ben Stormes, whose sister he married (Rita Lane Stormes).

TROY OVAL (D6)

Troy Oval was part of the Sassafras Hill Subdivision 91. It was dedicated as a street on January 6, 1969, in Ordinance 397-68. The developer stated that he named all his streets for aesthetic reasons only. The war between the Greeks and the Lord of Troy took place about the year 1183 B.C. Much of what you read about the Trojan Horse in Virgil's *Aeneid* is legend. Homer's *Odyssey* also mentions it. It, however, is very interesting reading. Could this street be named after one of the many cities in this country with the name? In the Albany, New York, area there is a relatively large city with a population of 54,000 by the name of Troy. Ohio has a city by that name in Miami County with a population of 19,000. Could someone have named this street after one of these cities?

TUCSON DRIVE (B3)

Tucson Drive was dedicated on September 19, 1966, in Ordinance 349-66. It was part of the Western Heights Development in which all the streets were named after western cities. This was appropriate enough inasmuch as the development was located on the far west side of Parma. The owners of the property were Norbert Malin and Sylvia Malin. It was developed by the Patricia Development Company.

TUXEDO AVENUE (E2)

Tuxedo Avenue has a very interesting history. It appears that it was originally named in Brooklyn Heights, Ohio. One resident related the oral history that early settlers from New York State were from the town called Tuxedo, New York (on the Hudson River in Orange County). The town, which gave its name to the formal dress suit called the tuxedo, gave this street its name. Tuxedo, New York, has quite a history which you might find interesting reading. I am told it has a museum dedicated to the tuxedo. E. Moran, the developer of what was called the Tuxedo Farms allotment, laid out North Street, Tuxedo Avenue and South Street. The street was dedicated apparently long after it was a street.

The date of dedication in Parma was May 4, 1922. It seems this street was around near Schaaf Road since the early 1900's. Mr. Moran set up other streets, such as Wexford Avenue, Marietta Avenue, Boston Avenue (later Grovewood Avenue) and Overlook Avenue (see Overlook Drive), later Brookdale Avenue. Early farmers in the area say Tuxedo Avenue may even go back into the 1800's. According to residents, the Dance Hall at the corner of Tuxedo Avenue and Schaaf Road in the early 1900's had nothing to do with the naming of Tuxedo Avenue. Tuxedo seems to have carried quite an influence into Parma. It worked its way all the way from Broadview Road to West 54th Street changing the street names of Beechway Avenue (September 21, 1925) and Herman Avenue (September 21, 1925) to Tuxedo Avenue.

TWIN LAKES DRIVE (D3)

This street was originally dedicated as Overland (Overlook) Drive on September 8, 1922, at the request of the Tuxedo Land Company. However, the persons owning lots in the area on November 9, 1925, in Ordinance 134, requested that the name of the street be changed from Overlook Road to Twin Lakes Drive. In the ordinance it says that Overland Drive ran from Homestead to Wooster Pike (Pearl Road). See Hampstead Drive for further information. In some legal documents the name was said to be Overlook Drive. There are two lakes running parallel with this street covering about five city blocks. They called them "Twin Lakes," from which the street gets it name.

Did you know that . . . .

The city of **Richmond Heights** was named after the Elihu Richmond family. They were one of the early settlers of this area. Richmond Heights was incorporated in 1917.

OHIO PLACE NAMES by Larry L. Miller
University of Indiana Press, 1996

V

VALEWOOD DRIVE (G3)

Valewood Drive was dedicated on July 19, 1965, in Ordinance 176-65 by Richard Subdivision #1. This subdivision is located by a wooded area with a deep valley containing Quarry Creek. It seems this would help explain the name given this street.

VALLEY VILLAS DRIVE (D7)

Valley Villas Drive is part of the Dogwood Estates and was dedicated on May 21, 1956, in Ordinance 104-56. The developer says that he picked the names because of the natural setting they would imply. This particular street had a very natural reason for its name. It is in an area of valleys and hills. Hidden Valley Lane, which is located in this secluded valley, is part of the Dogwood Estates also.

VALLEY LANE (D8)

Valley Lane is also part of the Dogwood Estates. It was dedicated on September 5, 1968. Valley Lane is a very small street that stops by the hills that form the Hidden Valley Estates off State Road. Though that developer says he picked names that were picturesque, this street has some real meaning behind its name.

VELMA AVENUE (D1)

This street was named after a descendent of the Krather Family. Velma Winter, for whom this street was named, had grandparents named Henry and Elizabeth Krather. Her mother was Susan Krather Koblenzer and her father was Christian Koblenzer. Her husband was Ralph Winter. Velma was born on February 17, 1897, and died on May 20, 1975. The Krathers were major property owners in the Brooklyn - Parma area. A street and large office building in Old Brooklyn bear the family name. Velma Avenue was dedicated on February 17, 1925. Information is from Luelda Gehring Schwab Barton, sister of Velma, on December 18, 1989, in her Old Brooklyn home. Information also came from county records Plat book, numbers

95 to 100, and long-time Parma resident Dr. Dudley Fay. (See picture 43.)

VICKSBURG DRIVE (G6)

Vicksburg Drive was dedicated on December 22, 1976, and on April 7, 1980, in Ordinance 166-79. It was named after the Civil War Battle of Vicksburg, Mississippi. This was suggested by a city official after he returned from a vacation visiting Civil War Memorials.

VILLE COURT (E7)

Ville Court was dedicated on January 6, 1969, in Ordinance 397-68. This was the Sassafras Hills Subdivision #1. Julius Paris, the developer, stated that most of his streets were named for aesthetic purposes. He used many French names (this word in French means town or city).

VINEWOOD DRIVE (G3)

Vinewood Drive was dedicated on July 19, 1965, in Ordinance 176-65 by Richard Subdivision #1. This Subdivision is located in a wooded area with a deep valley containing Quarry Creek. It appears to have been named for aesthetic purposes, which, at least in part, describes this area.

VIRGINIA AVENUE (D2)

Virginia Avenue was dedicated on September 13, 1919. The owners of the land were George and Minnie Friedrich, Emma Ball and W. L. Douglas, Ira D. and Barbara Siegfried. The developer was the Wooster Park Land Company. Despite extensive research, we had been unable to locate anyone who might have had this street named after her until we received a letter from Virginia Brown Fox from Tampa, Florida, who stated that this street was named after the daughter of Thomas B. Brown, Sales Director for H. A. Stahl Company. H. A. Stahl was Secretary of the Wooster Park Land Company, his initial start in Parma. A call was made to Mrs. Fox, and it was confirmed both by her and the detailed information received that this street was named after her, Virginia Brown Fox.

VISTA DRIVE (E7)

Vista Drive is a very short street off Sandy Hook Drive in the Woodbury Hills development. It is a street that stops just before the formation of a large valley. It is quite a natural setting for the residents. It was dedicated on November 16, 1964, in Ordinance 246-64.

VISTA LANE (D8)

Vista Lane is part of the Dogwood Estates. The developer said he used the names that seemed attractive to him and those with which people would be comfortable. Dogwood Estates is a very attractive residential area. The name says it all. Vista Lane was dedicated on February 20, 1967.

Did you know that . . . .

The town of **Glenwillow** was originally named Falls Junction. An early mayor didn't like that name and changed it to Willow Glen after a glen of willow trees in the area. Later the citizens changed it to Glenwillow because they liked the idea of one word for the name.

The city of **Gates Mills** was named after Halsey Mills, who settled here in 1812. He purchased property in 1826 and built a mill on it. The town was incorporated in 1924.

OHIO PLACE NAMES by Larry L. Miller
University of Indiana Press, 1996

WAINSTEAD DRIVE (D4)

This street was dedicated on December 12, 1923, at the request of H. A. Stahl, developer. He developed a large section of Parma and had great plans for the area. He named many of his streets after English place names from the Garden Cities. There is a town in southwest England in Cornwall County called Wainhouse Cor. The suffix "stead" emphasizes the previous symbol or word. For an explanation of H. A. Stahl's work, see "H. A. Stahl, A Tribute" in this book.

WAKE ROBIN DRIVE (C7)

Wake Robin Drive is a part of the Dogwood Estates. The developer, William DeGraeve, said he named these streets after birds and trees, names that would be attractive and where people would like to live. Wake Robin is not a bird as you might think; rather, it is a work published in 1899 about birds and nature by John Burroughs. It is a work of prose in which Mr. Burroughs gives his impressions of birds, animals and nature. Wake Robin Drive was dedicated on July 20, 1964, in Ordinance 162-64. Various nature centers, including the Metroparks Zoo, confirmed that there is no such bird as a Wake Robin.

WALES AVENUE (F3)

Wales Avenue was dedicated on April 11, 1923. It was part of the Wellington Park Allotments. Wales Avenue was also part of the Exeter Park Allotment by Don Helwick. The name Exeter is a popular name in Cleveland Heights, where there is an Exeter Road. He was a resident of Cleveland Heights and must have known others who lived in the Cleveland Heights-Shaker Heights area who were developing what were known, at that time, as the Garden Cities. Garden Cities were first developed in England and were special communities set aside from the big cities for what we would call suburban living. Mr. Helwick not only set up this community in this way by including valleys, parks and winding roads, but he also used the names found in these

Garden Communities. The above street is a good example. Wales is the name of a country on the British Isles. For more information, see "A Man with a Plan" in this book. The name "Wales" actually means the "enemy" or "other people." (Information is from *Place Names of the English Speaking World* by C. M. Matthews, page 296, and from County Plat Maps, County Room 216.) (See pictures 46 and 49.)

WALTER AVENUE (F2)

This street is named after the Jacob Walter Family. Jacob Walter started an ice business on a pond on his property; the business prospered for many years. He started it in 1890. In November 1968, Roy Walter witnessed the demolition of the ice plant which ended the ice business for the Walters. Later the pond became a grove and a park, which it is today. This street was dedicated on September 26, 1977 (Plat Vol. 129, page 25). However, the street was laid out on April 2, 1889, by the owner Jacob Walter. Members of the Walter Family still live on this street. We received information on the Walter family from Helen Kinkelaar, a relative of the Walter Family.

WARD ROAD (F7)

Ward Road was named after a very early family in Parma. It appears from the early maps that Sam Ward owned land in this area in 1852. His descendents, Daniel and Westley, owned land in the area on the 1892 maps. Daniel, however, owned the land where this road originates. Mr. Spuhler, who owns the Ward home now, says that the Wards had an 89-acre horse farm at this location.

WAREHAM ROAD (D4)

Wareham Road was dedicated on June 28, 1922. It was part of H. A. Stahl's Ridgewood Subdivision #5. Information on how Mr. Stahl named his streets can be seen in an earlier section in this book, "H. A. Stahl, A Tribute." This street possibly gets it name from the city of Wareham on the south central seacoast of England, about 30 miles from Southampton in Dorcet County. The Suffix "ham" refers to a homestead. So Wareham would be a Ware Family Homestead. Another town called Ware was a well-known market town in England, about 24 miles north of London on the Great North Road. (Information is from the County Plat Maps, Cuyahoga County Administration Building, and map of England.) (See picture 22.)

WARWICK DRIVE (E4)

This street was dedicated on June 28, 1922, at the request of H. A. Stahl. It was part of Ridgewood Subdivision #5. Information on how Mr. Stahl named his streets can be seen in an earlier section in this book called "H. A. Stahl, A Tribute." This street was possibly named after the city of Warwick in England, located about 15 miles south of Birmingham, England, in Warwickshire. Most of the streets that H. A. Stahl laid out were given English names. It might be noted that Robert, Earl of Warwick, was given the land that was later to become the state of Connecticut and that included the Western Reserve, of which Parma is part. (Information is from Ernie Kubasek's *History of Parma*, page 13.)

WELLINGTON AVENUE (E3)

Wellington Avenue was dedicated on July 12, 1922. It was a development of the Elworthy and Helwick Company. Wellington and other English names were used by Helwick to name his streets, many names of which were probably taken from the Garden City Directories. Garden Cities were created in the early 1900's for the wealthy so they could live in peace and luxury at the end of a hard day's work. Some sources say this directory was acquired by the VanSweringen brothers in setting up Shaker Heights. Exeter is the name Mr. Helwick used to set up his second subdivision of Wellington Avenue (1923). It is interesting because there is a town in southwest England, just north of Dartmoor National Park, called Exeter. There is also a street in Cleveland Heights by that name

(Exeter Road). From our investigation we discovered that most of these developers, including Mr. Helwick, lived in Shaker Heights and Cleveland Heights and must have been acquainted with each other's work, and it would appear all tried to create these Garden Cities areas down to the naming of the streets. To start with, the Duke of Wellington was the reason for this name; he was an outstanding British military leader in Europe and in India from 1799 into the 1800's. (For further information, see "A Man with a Plan" in the introduction of this book.) (See pictures 46 and 49.)

WENDY DRIVE (A8)

Many streets were named after admired and loved family members. This appears to be one of those streets. Wendy Drive was dedicated on September 2, 1958, in Ordinance 250-58 by Parma City Council for Marvin Gross, the developer. This street was named after Marvin's teenage daughter, Wendy Gross. Information is from Marvin Gross, the developer.

WESLEY DRIVE (D3)

Wesley Drive was dedicated on September 8, 1922. According to Dr. Dudley Fay, a descendent of the first settlers, the Wesley family married into the Kobelt family. The Kobelt family owned land and developed land in Parma in the late 1800's and early 1900's. The Kobelts owned land at the northeast section of Pearl and Snow Road (1903). The street named after the Wesley family is located at the southeast corner of Pearl and Snow Roads. Wesley Drive ran from Thorton Drive to Pearl Road. Later, on May 31, 1932, a major part of that street was changed to Chestnut Hills Drive, and only a little of Wesley Drive remains from Chestnut Hills Drive to Pearl Road.

WESTDALE DRIVE (A6)

Westdale Drive is a cross street located in the southwest corner of Parma. Appropriately named, it runs between Parma Park Boulevard and crosses Greenleaf Avenue, Beresford Avenue,

Oakwood Road and terminates at Maplewood Road. Westdale Drive was dedicated on October 7, 1957, in Parma City Ordinance 249-57.

WESTLAKE AVENUE (D2)

Westlake Avenue was dedicated on September 13, 1919. It was part of the Ridgewood Garden Allotment. The owners of the land were George and Minnie Friedrich, Emma Ball and W. L. Douglas and possibly Ira and Barbara Siegfried. Developers were the Wooster Park Land Company. No one has been able to say exactly why this street was named Westlake. Being on the west side of Cleveland at the time must have had something to do with the street being named Westlake. (Information is from County Plat Maps, Room 216.)

WEST PARKVIEW DRIVE (G6)

West Parkview Drive was dedicated on December 16, 1957, in Ordinance 340-57. West Parkview Drive is the continuation of Parkview Avenue. This street appears to have taken its name from the Quarry Creek, which is a very attractive park area on the east side of Parma. It is called West Parkview because it is on the west side of the Quarry Creek Valley. East Parkview is on the east side of the Quarry Creek. Parkview was the original street named, and it still holds to that name. However, it is the northern section of West Parkview Drive.

WEST 54TH STREET (E2)

We have not been dealing with "numbered streets" in this study unless a street has something special to add to our history. West 54th Street is one of those streets. West 54th street is one of Parma's busiest residential streets. It is a controversial street in that it is a three-lane street, but residents keep making it into a four-lane street, and city officials were reluctant to change the traffic flow because of its popularity as a four-lane street. However, in July 1998, West 54th was changed to a three-lane street. This is a main rush-hour artery going south from Brookpark Road. It was one of the original roads in Parma Village. It was a red-brick road for many years before it was black-topped. It ran from Brookpark to Ridgewood Golf Course until 1956, when it was extended to Orchard Park on July 30, 1956. This southern section was changed from West 54th to become part of Regency Drive on May 7, 1973, in Ordinance 231-72. It is a centrally located street so much so that Parma Senior High School was built on West 54th to serve all of Parma in the early 1950's. West 54th was the main north-south dividing line of property (1874 map) before it became a dedicated road. Maybe someday this street will become Howard A. Stahl Memorial Boulevard in honor of the man who put Parma on the map.

WEST 130TH STREET (A2)

This study does not include numbered streets unless they present a particular note of interest. West 130th would be just one of these streets. This street (the same continuous street) carries its number right through the county. This street was originally called Settlement Road. Later, in 1906, it became West 130th Street when streets in Cleveland received numbers. West 130th is one of the longest, if not the longest, numbered street in Cuyahoga County. It is the City of Parma's western city limits. Information is from Ernest Kubasek's *History of Parma*.

WESTMINSTER DRIVE (D4)

Westminster Drive was dedicated on December 12, 1923, by the township at the request of H. A. Stahl. As in all of H. A. Stahl planned developments, it is believed that he took the names of the streets from an English Directory of London's Garden Suburbs developed in the early 1900's. According to Cleveland's *Plain Dealer* (May 5, 1997), one of Parma's greatest public uproars in its history was over the proposed Parma Freeway in the 1960's and 1970's. It would have effectively taken out Westminster Drive as a residential street. Because of the uproar, the Freeway was never built. (For further information on this street and H. A. Stahl's work in Parma see "H. A. Stahl, A Tribute"

in this book.) The name Westminster literally translates to "the monastic church to the West." This name was given the church in London when it was built in the early seventh century on a marshy riverbank west of the city. Later, it became Westminster Abbey. It is located near Hyde Park on the River Thames. A company named Westminster Builders built on this street.

WESTMORELAND DRIVE (C2)

Westmoreland Drive is part of the Lake Park Allotments. These streets were developed by Frank Johnson, owner of the land. Westmoreland Drive was dedicated on August 28, 1919. There are two streets in Shaker Heights named Moreland: North Moreland and South Moreland. In the area near Lake Park Allotments, there was a development called Greenbriar Estates. The names of these streets appear to have been taken directly from Shaker Heights streets. Greenbriar Community was an upper class community. Westmoreland Drive seems to have been developed with this idea in mind. It is in a very attractive natural setting, part of which borders the Metroparks System.

WESTVIEW DRIVE (C2)

This street is located in the northwest section of Parma off the Big Creek Parkway near Brookpark Road. It was dedicated Westview Drive, appropriately, on June 18, 1953, in Ordinance 88-53. The Westview Apartments and the Knollwood Apartments are located in this area. The Big Creek Parkway makes this a very attractive area.

WEXFORD AVENUE (G2)

This is one of the few Irish names given to streets in Parma. Wexford was dedicated on April 28, 1922, and recorded on July 16, 1922. It is part of the E. Moran Tuxedo Farms Development. (Information was found in Cuyahoga County Plat Vol. 78, page 26.) Wexford is a town located in the southeast seacoast of Ireland and was a ninth century

Viking settlement. Though the Irish have adopted it, the name Wexford is a Viking name (Information is from *Place Names of the English Speaking World*, page 147, by C. M. Matthews.

WHIPPOORWILL LANE (C7)

Whippoorwill Lane was dedicated on February 20, 1967, in Ordinance 423-66. It is part of the Dogwood Estates. The streets in the Dogwood Estates were named after trees, birds, and nature areas. The developer said he picked the names he felt people would find comfortable to live with and for the natural setting they would suggest. Whippoorwill seems to fit that description. The whippoorwill is a night bird that sings "Whip-poor-will," which is how it got its name. If you have one in your neighborhood, you will know since it sings forever at night. These birds are our friends, as they eat night insects. They are not what you would call a beautiful bird; however, they do sing and some people enjoy that.

WHITAKER DRIVE (C7)

Whitaker Drive was originally dedicated on May 20, 1957, in Ordinance 107-57 as West 98th Street. Residents renamed the street Whitaker Drive on June 26, 1962, in Ordinance 79-62. According to some residents, the numbered street helped little in the location of the street. The name Whitaker was voted in by the residents. No resident among those involved in the voting could tell why the name Whitaker was picked. The person who picked the name had moved and is now deceased. The only person with that name who was quite popular in the 1960's was Roger Whitaker, an entertainer from London. (See picture 50.)

WHITEHAVEN DRIVE (D4)

Whitehaven Drive was dedicated on March 17, 1924, at the request of H. A. Stahl. H. A. Stahl named most of the streets he laid out after English places. They were generally towns or counties. Whitehaven is a city in England located on the Irish Sea, slightly northeast across the sea from Dublin, Ireland. It is just north of Liverpool, a seaport on England's west coast. (For further information on the reason for using English names see "H. A. Stahl, A Tribute" in this book.)

WHITTINGTON DRIVE (D3)

This street was dedicated on March 26, 1924, at the request of H. A. Stahl. It was in Ridgewood Allotment #2. Whittington is a settlement in England. There is also a man named Richard Whittington, who had a street named after him in London, apparently because his home (mansion) was razed for a marketplace and the people wanted to remember him. He was also Lord Mayor of London. He died in 1423. (Information is from *Place Names of the English Speaking World* by C. M. Matthews, page 36, and *Dictionary of City of London Street Names*, page 216, by Al Smith.) For further information see "H. A. Stahl, A Tribute" in this book.

WILBER AVENUE (D3)

Part of Wilber Avenue was dedicated on December 22, 1922, and part of it was dedicated on October 12, 1923, at the request of H. A. Stahl. Archbishop Joseph Schrembs, Bishop of the Diocese of Cleveland, was the owner of the property. This street has posed a problem to researchers. After checking with the Cleveland Diocese and city officials, we were unable to come up with an explanation for the name "Wilber." H. A. Stahl, the developer, named a couple of streets with male names. It is hard to see whom he might have named them after, as he had no children. However, some of his associates named a few streets after their children (see Kenneth Avenue). This could have been the cause for naming this street; however, this could not be verified. If anyone has any leads and knows something about the naming of this street, please contact the Historical Society of Parma.

WILLIAM CIRCLE (G5)

William Circle was dedicated on November 5, 1984, in Ordinance 115-84. This street was named after William Hoislbauer III. He is the grandson of William Hoislbauer I (1902 to 1989), who was owner and developer of the Rustic Trail Area; William Circle is part of this development.

WILLIAMSBURG DRIVE (G4)

Williamsburg Drive was dedicated on December 1, 1964, in Ordinance 271-64. It is one of a group of streets that were given names of patriotic locations in this country. Williamsburg is a historic, picture-book town of early colonial days. It is also the home of William and Mary College. Other streets in this development were Yorktown, Jamestown, Staunton and Winchester Drives. The developers were Fodor, Tilles and Miller.

WILLISTON DRIVE (E5)

Williston Drive was dedicated on September 5, 1967, in Ordinance 315-67. (Information came from Plat maps Vol. 200, pages 67-69.) Research has not uncovered any information as to why this street was called Williston. No one from the developer's office seemed to know why this street was called Williston Drive. There are a few people and places with this name. There is a village on Long Island called Williston Park with a 1950 population of 7,505. There was also a well-known professor from the University of Chicago and Kansas by the name of Sam Williston (1857 to 1918). There is a town in North Dakota called Williston City (population 7,378), the county seat of Williams County and also a trading center for cattle and wheat. If any one knows why this street was called Williston, please call the Parma Historical Society. (Information on names was obtained from sources at the Cuyahoga County Library, Parma Regional Branch.) (See picture 44.)

WINCHESTER DRIVE (G4)

Winchester Drive was dedicated on December 1, 1964, in Ordinance 172-64. This is a city in Virginia where two major Civil War battles were fought. The first was a Union defeat, but General Sheridan turned the second into a victory. Other streets in this subdivision named after patriotic locations were Jamestown Drive, Yorktown Drive, Williamsburg Drive and Staunton Drive. Developers were Fodor, Tilles and Miller. (See picture 41.)

WINDHAM DRIVE (B2)

Windham Drive was part of the Royal Park Subdivision. The street was dedicated on August 24, 1927. An interesting item that might be mentioned here is that Moses Cleaveland, the founder of the City of Cleveland, was from Windham County in Connecticut. This street was dedicated with Brainard Drive, which was named after a local family. Nothing has been found that would indicate why this street was named as such. Windham Drive joins Brainard Drive just before Hauserman Road. It gives a very attractive appearance.

WINTERPARK DRIVE (G8)

Winterpark Drive was dedicated by City Council on April 17, 1961, in Ordinance 57-61. It is one of the streets of the so-called Florida Estates. These streets were named after Florida cities at the suggestion of Councilman-at-large James Day (soon to be elected mayor) after he returned from a trip to Florida. Winter Park is a city in Florida just outside Orlando. There were actually two developments named after Florida locations; one was between Pleasant Valley Road and Sprague Road west of Broadview Road, and the other one was between Pleasant Valley Road and Sprague Road, east of State Road.

WINTHROP DRIVE (F4)

Winthrop Drive was named after John Winthrop, a political figure in the pilgrim colony in Massachusetts. He was a member of the pilgrim family from which other streets in the area got their names. The street was dedicated on November 21, 1927. (See Alden Drive for more information.) (See picture 40.)

WOLF AVENUE (D2)

Wolf Avenue was dedicated on December 27, 1927. According to Dr. Dudley Fay, an elderly resident (6-28-89) and a descendant of the original first settlers of Parma, Wolf Avenue was named after the Carl Wolf family, who owned the land where this street is located. Other members of the family were George, Mabel, Harvey and Evelyn. (Information is from County maps, Book 113-114, page 36, and Dr. Dudley Fay.) (See picture 48.)

WOOD AVENUE (E2)

Wood Avenue was dedicated on May 1, 1920. It was part of the Lookout Heights Subdivision. Conger and Helper were the developers. This street appears to have been named after a general in the First World War. He was General Leonard Wood. Tony Dalesio furnished this hypothesis. Since Wood Avenue is located in the area where there are other streets named after generals in the First World War (Liggett and Pershing), it seems quite logical, especially when we consider the name of the subdivision ("Lookout"). Pershing Avenue was in this Subdivision. Tony Dalesio is a resident of Parma and has a love of history, especially the history of the First World War. See Liggett Drive for further information.

WOOD THRUSH DRIVE (E5)

Wood Thrush Drive is a relatively new street. It was dedicated on April 18, 1988, in City Ordinance 294-87. The wood thrush is a bird. These birds are woodland birds; they have a clear flute-like sound and have a heavily spotted breast. They eat insects and are ant eaters. Sounds like a nice bird to have around. This was part of the Joseph Dzurilla Subdivision #2.

WOODBURY HILLS DRIVE (E7)

Woodbury Hills Drive was part of the Woodbury Hills Subdivision. The street was dedicated on April 16, 1962, in Ordinance 38-62. The English meaning of "bury" is a fortification or stronghold. Therefore Canterbury was a fortified town called Canter. So Woodbury would refer to a fortification made of wood. Of course, that doesn't sound as romantic as Woodbury, but names have a way of becoming romanticized through the years.

WOODLANDS BOULEVARD (D8)

Woodlands Boulevard is part of the Pine Tree Subdivision #1. It was dedicated on June 15, 1992, in City Ordinance 63-92. According to developer and engineer Richard MacKay, this street and all the other streets in this development were named after golf courses. Besides other places, there is a Woodlands Golf Course in Wayne, Michigan. Other streets in this development are Ironwood Circle, Tanglewood Lane, Oakwood Oval, and Highland Hills Court.

WOODLAWN DRIVE (F4)

Woodlawn Drive was dedicated on May 24, 1965, in City Ordinance 112-65. It is part of the Richard Subdivision #2. This street is not immediately visible to the residents of Parma, as it runs off West 29th Street, a short distance from the beautiful Quarry Creek Valley. This street truly lives up to its name. Information is from the City Engineer's office.

WOODROW AVENUE (E4)

Woodrow Avenue was dedicated on April 21, 1924. The V. F. W. Hall is located on this street. President Woodrow Wilson, who died on February 3, 1924, was president from 1913 to 1921. Given the above circumstances, it is a good assumption the street was named after him. An extensive effort was made to locate someone at the V. F. W. Hall who might know, but no one could be found. The owners of the land were

George and Sarah Loesch (between West 48th Street and State Road). The extension of Woodrow Avenue came on May 14, 1962.

WOODWAY AVENUE (Fl)

Woodway Avenue was part of the Brook-State Subdivision and was dedicated on April 20, 1918. It was part of the property owned by the Henningers and Uhincks. There is no one around who can tell us why the name Woodway was used, but it appears the name might have been used to describe the area. Parma was a wooded area in the early days, and this might have been a good description of this area. Woodway Avenue winds from Tuxedo Avenue, down a slight grade, and meets West 45th and West 44th on a curve and then runs into a very attractive area at the intersection of Roseside and Daleside Drives.

WOOSTER PARKWAY (D2)

Wooster Parkway, in all probability, received its name from the Wooster Pike (Pearl Road). Wooster Parkway runs between Ridge into Pearl Road (Wooster Pike before 1927). Wooster Parkway was dedicated on December 18, 1919. Wooster Pike received its name because it was a road (Pike) to Wooster, Ohio. (See Pearl Road for more information.) There was a Revolutionary General named David Wooster (1711 to 1777). He was killed in the Revolutionary War. It would be quite a privilege to have this name for your street.

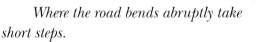

Streets and Roads . . . .

Where the road bends abruptly take short steps.

Ernest Bramah
"Golden Hours"
pg. 169-14

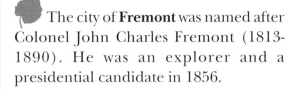

Did you know that . . . .

The city of **Fremont** was named after Colonel John Charles Fremont (1813-1890). He was an explorer and a presidential candidate in 1856.

The city of **Cambridge**, Ohio, was named by the early settlers who were from Cambridge, Maryland. The town was laid out in 1806 by Zacheus Beatty and Jacob Gomber. It was incorporated in 1837.

The city of **Bratenahl** was named after Charles Bratenahl who was a landowner along the Lake Erie shore in this area. He settled here in the mid 1800's. The town was incorporated in 1904.

The city of **Dayton** was named after Honorable Jonathan Dayton (1760-1824), an early landowner. He had quite a military and political career. Dayton was incorporated in 1805.

The city of **Rittman**, Ohio, was named after the treasurer of the Atlantic and Great Western Railroad, Frederick B. Rittman. Rittman was incorporated in 1911.

The town of **Roscoe** was named after an English historian and author, William Roscoe (1753-1831). It was originally called Caldersburg in 1816 after James Calder, who laid out the town.

OHIO PLACE NAMES by Larry L. Miller
University of Indiana Press, 1996

YORK ROAD (C6)

York Road was dedicated on June 28, 1926. According to the *History of Parma* by Ernest R. Kubasek, this street was named by early settlers from New York State. It was originally called York Street. Township records, however, refer to this street on February 27, 1909. This is a possibility, as some streets were in existence years before their dedication. (Information was obtained from County Plat Maps, Vol. 191, page 80.)

YORKSHIRE ROAD (E3)

This street was dedicated on July 12, 1922, by Parma Township at the request of Elworthy and Helwick, developers. It appears that Helwick and Elworthy might have been acquainted with H. A. Stahl, who developed Parma Circle. The name of this street could have been chosen the same way the names were chosen for Parma Circle streets. (See Introduction for further information on this street.) In any case, there is a County in England, Yorkshire County (shire), where the city of York is located, for which this street has been named. Wellington Avenue was also developed with this street.

YORKTOWN DRIVE (G4)

This street was named after Yorktown, Virginia. This town was the site of the final battle for American independence, which occurred on October 14, 1781. This and a number of other streets in this area were given names of towns and places for which American independence was fought. Yorktown Drive was dedicated on December 1, 1964, in City Ordinance 172-64. The developers were Fodor, Tilles and Miller.

ZONA LANE (A7)

Zona Lane was named after a former Mayor of Parma, Stephen A. Zona. He had a distinguished career. He served 39 years as a public servant. He was 21 years old as a state legislator and served six years as Mayor of Parma, from 1952 to 1958. He was a Judge at Parma Municipal Court when he died in 1969. Information was provided by former Mayor James Day. Zona Lane was dedicated on February 4, 1957, in Ordinance 24-57.

Streets and Roads . . . .

*Because the road was steep and long
And through a dark and lonely land,*

God set upon my lips a song and put a lantern in my hand

**Joyce Kilmer,
"Love's Lantern", pg. 1879-5**

Thus says the Lord: Stand beside the earliest roads, ask the pathways of old Which is the way to good, and walk it; thus you will find rest for your souls.

(Jeremiah 6:16a)

*Great roads the Romans built that men might meet
And walls to keep strong men apart, secure
Now centuries are gone, and in defeat
The walls are fallen, but the road endure*

**Ethelyn Miller Hartwich
"What Shall Endure?"**

APPENDIX

MADISON COUNTRY CLUB
AND COMMUNITY FOR A REAL SUMMER VACATION

One of H. A. Stahl's great achievements was the Madison Country Club and Resort Area. The resort and country club was to serve Western Pennsylvania and Northeast Ohio. In the original brochure it was described as a "summer home colony of refinement and distinction." It was unique in that its membership was restricted to resident owners in what was called the Madison Golf Lakelands. It was for the people who would like to spend their summer vacations in a summer home on Lake Erie in a community that "offered every facility for rest and relaxation" and who liked golfing. The 27-hole golf course and country club was set up for casual and luxury living. There were dining rooms and large screened-in areas where people could come in from the lake, their summer homes or right off the golf course to enjoy themselves together .There were many activities at the country club. There were exquisite dances weekly. One resident described it as having a holiday once a week, every Saturday night. The country club was the center of activity in this area. Today the screened area has been turned into a large dining room with nothing but the best food and service. Mr. Stahl would approve of this outstanding community facility.

This community was what was called in the 1920's a summer resort. The cottages, as he called them, were actually not cottages as we know them but homes with summer attractions such as large screened-in porches and large shaded areas. Mr. Stahl had designed his streets with rows of trees of various kinds such as birches, sycamores and maples. Today these trees form beautiful arches over the streets - a beauty that has to be seen to be appreciated. This kept the hot summer sun off the homes when there was no air conditioning. Today most people live there year round and it has developed into a mixture of high class living to middle-income residents. The homes border on Lake Erie so the residents have the opportunity to use the lake as they would like. Stahl had planned a beautiful beach park for the whole community along the lake shore. Today one can see that there has been a lot of beach erosion and the individual homes on the lake have taken over some of the beaches.

As usual, this is another community where H. A. Stahl put his whole effort into developing a community people could enjoy. Putting his money back into the community in this effort.

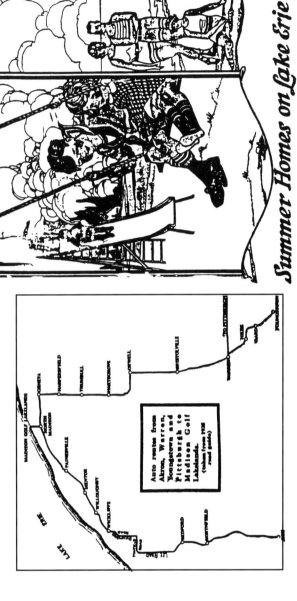

Madison Lakelands

Summer Homes on Lake Erie

The H. A. Stahl Properties Company

Owners and Developers of

Madison Golf Lakelands

Ridgewood

Cleveland Heights
at Lakeland, Fla.

High grade recreational and residence communities

OFFICERS

H. A. Stahl, President
W. L. Dupplin, Vice-President
R. M. Beckford, Secy. & Treas.

DIRECTORS

T. C. Brown   O. C. Little
E. H. Rogers   J. E. Mansfield
C. E. Hatch   H. R. Neel
F. D. Kellogg   H. J. Neel
E. H. Kramer   A. E. Reamer
J. C. Anders

Auto routes from Akron, Warren, Youngstown and Pittsburgh to Madison Golf Lakelands
(taken from road guide)

MADISON, An Institution

MADISON Golf Lakelands is an institution. It was conceived and created as a summer home colony of refinement and distinction and the high ideals which were established in the beginning have been adhered to rigidly and regardless of ulterior considerations.

We took Madison Golf Lakelands in its virgin state three years ago with its woods, its meadows and its fallow farming land stretching for a mile along beautiful Lake Erie and transformed it into a residential play spot — not too high priced for the average man, yet complete in every detail of appointment. We restricted the membership to owners of land and only those selected by invitation may buy and build homes within its borders.

Some thought our ambition was too high, but time has shown, and the personnel of the present membership is living proof of the need for a recreational community such as Madison Golf Lakelands is today. Every season emphasizes its importance and prestige—every day it becomes more essential and its value increases.

Madison offers every facility for rest and relaxation. If it appeals to you don't hesitate. You will be rewarded through the joy of living in the fresh air and freedom of the great outdoors among congenial people. And you will be sure, furthermore, that your investment will enhance in value more and more as the years go by.

President.

COPY OF BROCHURE FURNISHED BY THE MADISON COUNTRY CLUB

BROCHURE FURNISHED BY THE CLEVELAND HEIGHTS COUNTRY CLUB, LAKELAND, FLORIDA

H. A. STAHL — President
W. L. DOUGLASS — Vice-President
R. E. POWER — Vice-President
J. H. REDING — Vice-President
B. M. BECKSTED — Sec'y & Treas.
T. J. HOULIHAN — Asst. Secretary

DIRECTORS

B. M. BECKSTED
Sec'y Treas., H. A. Stahl Properties Co., Cleveland.

T. B. BROWN
Director of Sales, H. A. Stahl Properties Co., Cleveland.

W. L. DOUGLASS
Vice-Pres., H. A. Stahl Properties Co., Cleveland.

J. J. HALDEMAN
President, Lakeland Realty and Mortgage Co., Lakeland.

F. D. KELLOGG
Vice-Pres. and Treas., Ohio Quarries Co., Cleveland.

E. H. KRUEGER
Attorney and President Fidelity Mortgage Co., Cleveland.

HERMAN R. NEFF
President, Geo. S. Rider Company, Cleveland.

HERMAN NORD
Attorney, Cleveland.

C. S. PELTON
President, Perfection Heater C Cleveland.

R. E. POWER
Vice-Pres. and Director of Pub ity, H. A. Stahl Florida Prop ties Co.

J. C. SANDERS
Vice-Pres., Union Trust C Cleveland.

W. A. C. SMITH
President, Ohio Quarries Compa Cleveland.

TRIS SPEAKER
Manager, Cleveland Baseball Clu

H. A. STAHL
President, H. A. Stahl Properti Co., Cleveland.

OFFICES

Lakeland, Fla.
St. Petersburg, Fla.
Tampa, Fla.
Cleveland, Ohio.

106 South Tennessee A
532-534 Central A
Crescent Apte., Lafayette St., W
Sixth Floor Hickox Bl

DEPOSITORIES

First National Bank, Lakeland, Florida
State Bank of Lakeland, Lakeland, Florida
Central National Bank Savings and Trust Co., Cleveland, Ohio

A Responsible Company

The H. A. Stahl Properties Co, established at Cleveland in 1912, is an experienced and financially responsible corporation, which has successfully created, developed and operated several high-class residential and country club properties, Madison Golf Lakelands, on Lake Erie near Cleveland, with two golf courses, half a mile of beach, a magnificent clubhouse, tennis and roque courts, riding stables, etc., is nationally known for its high grade character and excellence. The Stahl Company also owns Ridgewood, a new home and recreational development at Cleveland, covering 1,250 acres with playgrounds, lakes, 18-hole championship golf course and every modern improvement. Over two-third of Ridgewood's 7,000 lots are already sold.

Cleveland Heights

Lakeland, Florida

A HIGHLY RESTRICTED RESIDENTIAL GOLF AND COUNTRY CLUB DEVELOPMENT

GOLF CARD

Nº	Out YDS.	In	
1	333	10	337
2	415	11	317
3	263	12	173
4	450	13	443
5	420	14	477
6	117	15	367
7	394	16	377
8	462	17	228
9	353	18	380
	3207		3099

TOTAL – 6306.

Directions by Street Car

West 25th car from Public Square to Car Barns, change to Ridge and Pearl Rd. car, which goes direct to clubhouse.

By Auto

From Public Square to Central Viaduct, out 14th St. to Clark Ave., turn right on Clark Ave. to Scranton Rd., turn left on Scranton Rd. Follow same to W. 25th St., continue straight out 25th to Ridge Rd., then bear left with car line direct to club house.

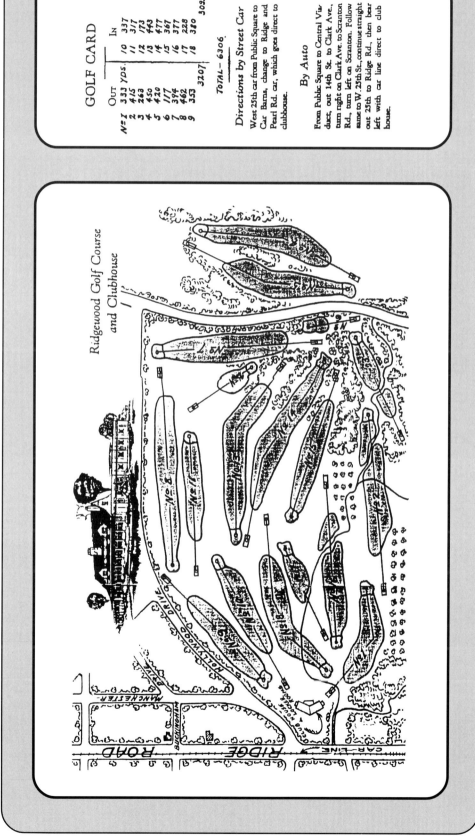

Ridgewood Golf Course and Clubhouse

Ridgewood the Beautiful

Ridgewood Golf Links is laid out in the tree-covered hills and valleys between Ridge and Bean Roads, eight miles southwest of Public Square. With the exception of the Country Club in Brecksville, it is the closest to the business district of any golf course in Cleveland.

The course was designed by Grange Alves, professional at Acacia Club, and built by the Stahl engineers. Every modern feature was incorporated in the layout including creeping bent greens of velvety texture.

The scenic beauty of Ridgewood is simply marvelous, due to the hilly character of the land and the magnificent trees and flowering shrubs which were left to remain in their native splendor. In fact, Ridgewood is so clean and secluded that one has a feeling of being a long, long way from the city instead of only 20 minutes ride.

Because of its character, Ridgewood is ideal to entertain groups of golfing friends or business associates who are frowned upon as guests at private clubs. You can enjoy every facility of the private club, caddies, lockers, showers, good food, iced drinks, etc., at a minimum of expense. The sporty course is a real test of golf with a great variety of holes and splendid putting greens. Its natural beauty is unusual and its attractiveness and easy accessibility quite unusual.

Owned and operated by
The H. A. Stahl Properties Co.
Hickox Building, Cleveland, Ohio

Hello:

Great:

RIDGEWOOD ~ Where You Pay As You Play

Ideal for Golfers of Moderate Means

One of the sportiest and most beautiful golf courses in Ohio.

20 minutes from the business center of Cleveland.

Beautiful creeping bent greens and tree-lined fairways.

All the attractions of a private club without the cost.

No initiation fee—no dues—no assessments.

Starting times reserved by telephone. Simply phone the clubhouse, Lincoln 3892.

Ridgewood was designed by Grange Alves and built by Stahl engineers—it's a scientific layout.

Ridgewood was opened for play July 4, 1925.

Ridgewood has a fine clubhouse with two spacious locker rooms, showers, restaurant, lounge and soda grill.

Everybody Welcome at Ridgewood

It is not necessary to be a property owner to play golf at Ridgewood. No restrictions are placed upon those who play except the payment of a small daily fee and this fee includes lockers and showers and the free use of the clubhouse in every particular.

COMPARING RIDGEWOOD COMMUNITY TO WELWYN GARDEN CITY COMMUNITY

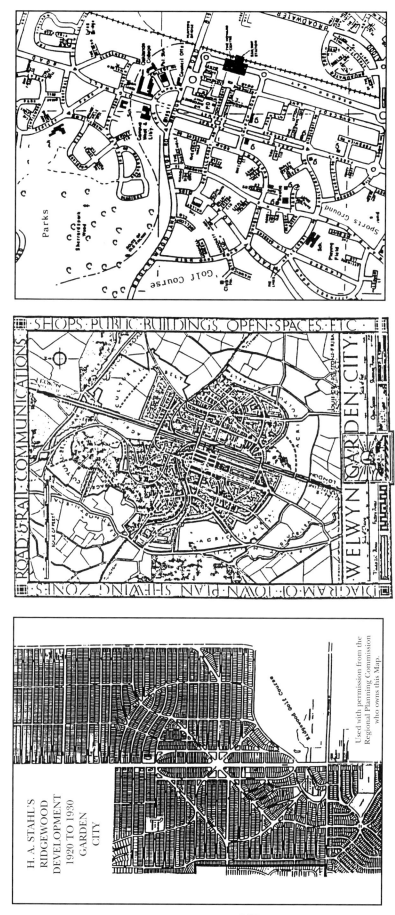

WELWYN GARDEN CITY
PRESENT DAY

1920 TOWN PLAN

1920's

Used with permission from the
Regional Planning Commission
who owns this Map.

H. A. STAHL'S
RIDGEWOOD
DEVELOPMENT
1920 TO 1930
GARDEN
CITY

Welwyn Garden City is a suburban Garden City of London, England.

It was planned and developed in the 1920's

CREDITS

DAVE NESTER

I would like to give special recognition to DAVE NESTER of the City of Parma Engineer's Office for his generosity in going out of his way to help in this project. Thanks, Dave.

PATRICIA DAVIS

I would also like to give special recognition to Patty Davis of Cowgill Printing for her help and advice.

A SPECIAL THANKS TO:

James W. Day — Former Mayor of Parma for his invaluable knowledge

John Petruska — Former Mayor of Parma for his suggestions and help in coming up with some answers to some difficult questions.

Mayor Gerald Boldt — For his interest and help

James Ptacek — County Public Information Office

Gregory Payne — County Public Information Office

Sherri Mangay — Cuyahoga County Public Library

Dorothy Loebs — For her suggestions

Ernest Kubasek — For his suggestions and the use of his book, *The History of Parma*

Danny Panek — Golf Pro, Ridgewood Country Club

Ann K. Sindelar — Western Reserve Historical Society for their invaluable pictures

Judith Cetina — Cuyahoga County Archives

Laura McShane — for the Quarry Creek Study and the CRCPO

TRW-Redi Company — for the use of their maps

Sharon Alexander — for her proof reading and advice

A BIG THANK YOU TO:

Angelo Callari — Club Manager, Ridgewood Country Club

Tom Breckenridge — Cleveland *Plain Dealer*

Debbie Palmer — *Parma Sun Post*

Eleanor Fanslau — Sam Miller's Office, Forest City Inc.

Richard MacKay — MacKay Engineer & Surveying Co.

Charles McKinney — McKinney-McCann Associates

Ted Aldrich — Informant at Madison Country Club

Carol Clary	Cuyahoga County Library, Parma Regional
Lee Frierson	Director, Cleveland Heights Golf Course
	Lakeland, Florida
Harrison Gleasons	Friends of the Stahls
Gilbert George	Resident
Claudia Helwick	Daughter-in-law to Don Helwick
Randy Owoc	Manager, Madison Country Club
William Snack	Resident
Bruce Young	From his collection - Aerial photos 1949
Robert Runyan	Photographer - Aerial photos 1949
Rosemary Rein	Madison Country Club
Terry Burns	Cuyahoga County Library, Parma Regional
Melanie Deutsch	Cuyahoga County Library, Parma Regional
Yvette Grants	Cuyahoga County Library, Parma Regional
John Bellamy	Cuyahoga County Library, Fairview Branch
Elaine Swade	Clerk's Office, City of Parma
Bernie Survoy	Clerk of Council, Parma
Margaret Noll	Resident
Lois Hajek	Resident
George Hajek	Resident
Duane Whittenberger	Resident
Eleanor Sadowski	Resident
Sophie Senko	Resident
Elaine Obloy	Cuyahoga County Library, Parma Regional
Nancy Pazelt	Cuyahoga County Library, Parma Regional
Karin Weinhold	Cuyahoga County Library, Parma Regional
Roseanne Ziefle	Parma's Planning Commission Secretary
Virginia Brown Fox	Her father was in Sales Department for H. A. Stahl
Dan Spangler	Mogadore Cemetery, Mogadore, Ohio
Charles Wagner	Forest City, Residential Development
Marvin Gross	Developer
Mogadore City Hall	Helping on research
Richard MacKay	MacKay Engineer and Survey Company

University of Indiana Press and Larry L. Miller, author, for the use of material
in their book *Ohio Place Names* in the "Did you know" articles that
appeared in this book.

And all the others who have helped through the years for whatever reason
I have been unable to name here. Thank you very much.

Hats off and a big thank you to

Cowgill Printing Company

(one of Parma's oldest established businesses)

for a great job in printing this publication;

their cooperation and advice

were immensely helpful in putting this book together.